TONY BENNETT
ONSTAGE *and in the* STUDIO

TONY BENNETT
ONSTAGE *and in the* STUDIO

TONY BENNETT *–with–* **DICK GOLDEN**

Foreword by Michael Bublé
Preface by Danny Bennett

STERLING
New York

STERLING
New York

An Imprint of Sterling Publishing Co., Inc.
1166 Avenue of the Americas
New York, NY 10036

ISBN 978-1-4549-3124-9

Distributed in Canada by Sterling Publishing Co., Inc.
c/o Canadian Manda Group, 664 Annette Street
Toronto, Ontario M6S 2C8, Canada
Distributed in the United Kingdom by GMC Distribution Services
Castle Place, 166 High Street, Lewes, East Sussex BN7 1XU, England
Distributed in Australia by NewSouth Books
45 Beach Street, Coogee, NSW 2034, Australia

For information about custom editions, special sales, and premium and
corporate purchases, please contact Sterling Special Sales at 800-805-5489 or
specialsales@sterlingpublishing.com.

Manufactured in Canada

2 4 6 8 10 9 7 5 3 1

sterlingpublishing.com

Interior design by Lorie Pagnozzi
Picture credits – See page 184

"TO ME, **LIFE IS A GIFT**, AND IT'S A BLESSING TO JUST BE ALIVE. AND EACH PERSON SHOULD LEARN WHAT A GIFT IT IS **TO BE ALIVE** NO MATTER HOW TOUGH THINGS GET."

– TONY BENNETT

CONTENTS

foreword

BEFORE I EVER GOT THE CHANCE TO MEET
TONY BENNETT, I WAS ONE OF MANY MILLIONS
OF FANS WHO HAD FALLEN IN LOVE WITH
HIS VOCAL PROWESS AND UNIQUE SOUND.
AS A SINGER, I HAD ALWAYS BEEN KEENLY
AWARE OF HOW IMPORTANT IT WAS TO HAVE
AN INSTRUMENT THAT WAS COMPLETELY AND
UTTERLY DISTINCT.

WHEN YOU HEAR A VOICE COMING OUT
OF THE RADIO, DO YOU KNOW WITHIN A
BAR OF MUSIC WHO YOU ARE LISTENING TO?
THE ANSWER WITH TONY WAS ALWAYS A
RESOUNDING *YES.*

My grandparents had emigrated from Italy, and as a proud Canadian of Italian extraction, you can imagine how popular the songs of Frank, Dino, and Tony were in our household. I can remember being around eight years old and belting out songs like "I Left My Heart in San Francisco" and "The Good Life."

The music and singers of the Great American Songbook were always the soundtrack to our family's life.

Long before my dream of becoming a professional singer had come true, I had already recognized the incredible power, range, and singular tone of Tony's voice. Years later, after embarking on a career of my own, I found myself on a world tour and staying in a beautiful hotel in Venice. While I was in the hotel gym for a workout, who happened to be running on the treadmill next to me? Only one of my childhood heroes . . . the one and only Tony Bennett! As you might imagine, I was thrilled.

What made it even more special to me was that after I introduced myself, Mr. Bennett (always warm, gracious, and kind) told me that he was a fan of mine!

As someone who holds this genre of music in such high regard, I can honestly tell you that no greater compliment could have been bestowed upon me. One of the greatest performers who ever lived gave me one of the most significant moments of my life. . . . His acceptance meant a hell of a lot to me. In the many years to come, his friendship would mean even more.

Fast-forward to 2006. I'm in Capitol Studios in Los Angeles, standing outside the double doors that lead to the recording room. I am about to sing one of my favorite Tony Bennett songs with the Man himself—a duet of "Just in Time." As I open the door and peek inside, I am filled with a jolt of nervousness mixed with excitement as I see we will be recording live off the floor with the boys in Tony's band!

Up to that point of my career, the producers I had worked with had always cut the band separately and I added vocals to the finished tracks. Recording with Tony and his quartet that day changed my way of thinking about making records and inspired me as an artist. I left that session knowing this was how I would record my own music for the rest of my life.

Tony had given me a great gift that day.

To be honest, he had always been quick to share advice or his opinion on music if he thought it might help me. One of my favorite anecdotes to share was when he told me, "If you steal from one person you're a thief, but when you steal from everyone, you can call it research."

The thought of him saying that with a sly grin on his face and a little chuckle always makes me smile. It's great advice, too, by the way.

* * *

OVER THE YEARS, I'VE BEEN HONORED to perform with Tony many times. One of the most special was being asked to appear at his ninetieth birthday celebration, which was held at Radio City Music Hall in 2016.

More than a decade after my first of many performances with him, this time, I got to perform for him. As he sat in the front row, it was a very emotional moment for me. I wanted very badly to convey how much he meant to me—both as a fan and as a performer. I have cherished my long friendship and association with Tony, as he has always been an inspiration. I had hoped my performance that night would capture the genuine sense of respect and admiration I have held for him all these years.

I honestly sang with so much love that night, and was deeply moved as I looked out into the audience to see Tony and his wife standing as my performance had come to an end. I took a bow and thought to myself, "Wow! . . . Just another life-changing moment Tony had been part of gifting me."

Later that evening, at ninety years old, Tony took the stage and closed the show. It was pure magic. And, as he has been known to do, before he began his ultimate rendition of "Fly Me to the Moon" Tony asked the sound engineer to turn off his microphone. Six thousand adoring audience members were suddenly breathless.

Tony filled the cavernous theater with the awesome and raw power of his voice. The intense power was only matched by the strength of his conviction.

After a long, standing ovation, as the silence ensued, he grinned and with that twinkle in his eye, looked out into his adoring audience and said, "I love you."

Well, Tony, this is my chance to say it back.

I love you, Tony.

—*Michael Bublé*

Michael Bublé at the "Tony Bennett Celebrates 90" concert at Radio City Music Hall, September 15, 2016.

"I HAVE CHERISHED MY LONG FRIENDSHIP AND ASSOCIATION WITH TONY, AS HE HAS ALWAYS BEEN AN INSPIRATION. I HAD HOPED MY PERFORMANCE THAT NIGHT WOULD CAPTURE THE GENUINE SENSE OF RESPECT AND ADMIRATION I HAVE HELD FOR HIM ALL THESE YEARS."

—MICHAEL BUBLÉ

preface

"MUSIC IS EITHER GOOD OR IT'S BAD. IT'S NOT MY OPINION—IT'S A FACT!" THAT'S A PHRASE MY FATHER PROUDLY PROCLAIMED FOR AS LONG AS I CAN REMEMBER. BEING A CHILD OF THE SIXTIES, IT WAS PARTICULARLY HARD FOR ME TO WRAP MY HEAD AROUND THAT NOTION. I ALWAYS CONSIDERED ARTISTIC TASTE TO BE SUBJECTIVE AND, QUITE FRANKLY, *TRULY* A MATTER OF OPINION.

I GREW UP IN A HOUSEHOLD IMMERSED IN MUSIC AND ART. MY FATHER WAS A SINGER AND A PAINTER, AND MY MOTHER WAS A VISUAL ARTIST IN HER OWN RIGHT. MY BROTHER, DAEGAL, AND I WERE EXPOSED ON A DAILY BASIS TO THE MOST EXTRAORDINARY AND TALENTED MUSICIANS.

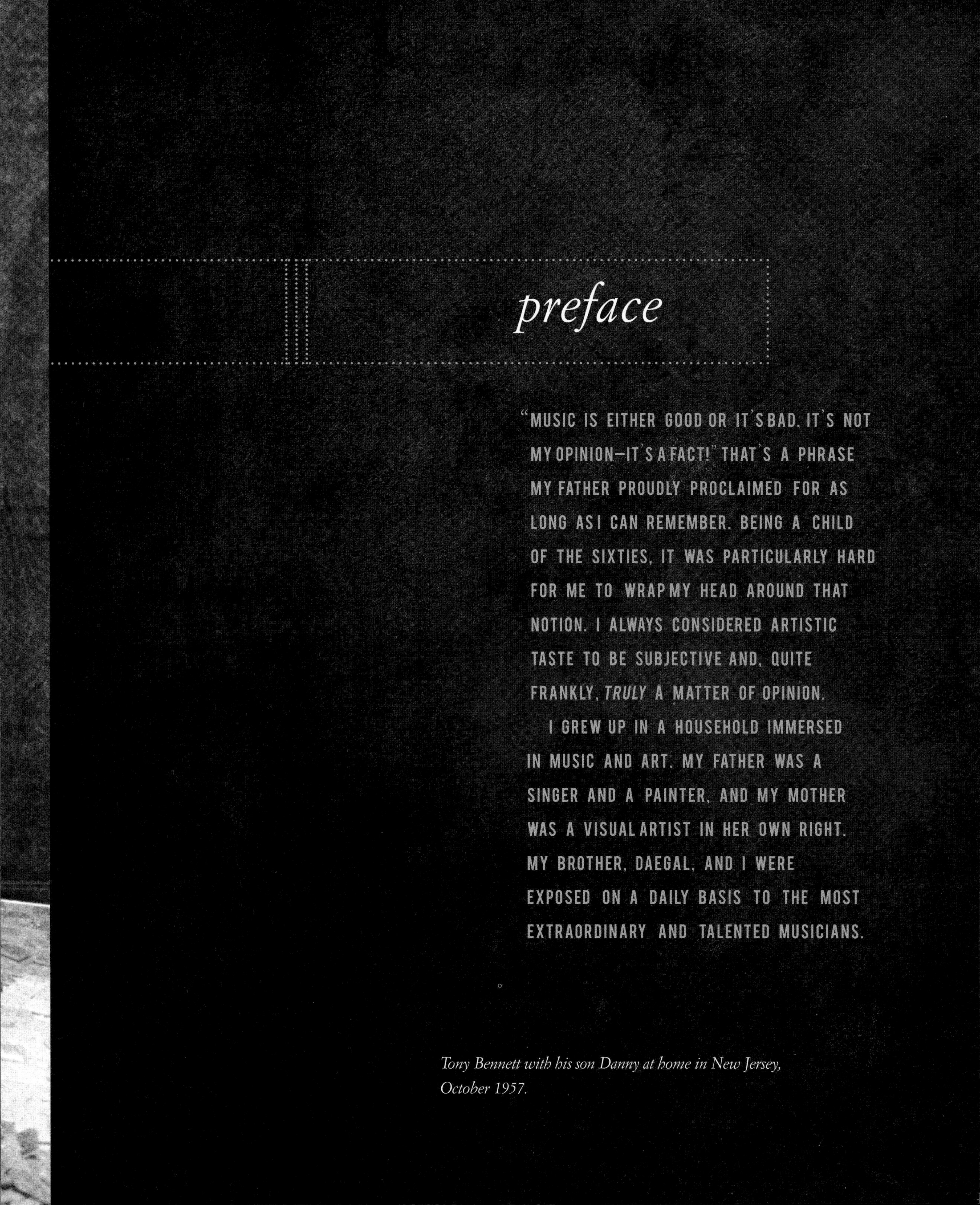

Tony Bennett with his son Danny at home in New Jersey, October 1957.

Duke Ellington, Ella Fitzgerald, Count Basie, and Dizzy Gillespie, to name a few, were like aunts and uncles to us. In fact, many nights after my dad's recording sessions would begin at the Columbia Records recording studios in Manhattan they would often continue into the early hours of the morning in the basement of our house in Englewood, New Jersey, a short jaunt from Midtown. At times, Dae and I would be woken in the middle of the night by the sweet strains of Bobby Hackett's coronet or the mellow sax sounds of Stan Getz. We would carefully sneak to the top of the stairs and listen in wonder.

In 1979, I was twenty-seven, and I got a call from my dad who was living in Los Angeles at that time. He was going through a pretty rough period and asked if Dae and I would fly out to see him as he had some important things he wanted to discuss with us. We caught the next flight out to the West Coast and met him at his house in Beverly Hills. It was a beautiful homestead with all the L.A. trimmings, but typically Tony preferred to spend most of his time in his painting studio, which was a well-appointed converted bathhouse by the pool.

He did not have a manager at the time, and he told us that he felt things were coming apart at the seams. He felt directionless and asked if we would look things over and make some suggestions as to what he should do next. We of course said we would do our best, and thus began this amazing journey together that has lasted now for forty years.

Although Dae and I had been in working rock bands since we were young kids smitten by the Beatles, I also had this bizarre obsession about finding out everything I could about the music business. I read and absorbed any new article I could find regarding the industry as well as studied any existing music-related litigation or contracts I could get my hands on. So it didn't take me too long to understand my dad's current state of business affairs and what was needed to get things back on track. My role as Tony's manager evolved over time. Above all else, I wanted to make sure that we were able to effectively separate the business from our personal life, which, of course, isn't an easy feat. I instinctively knew that in order for this to work, I would have to earn my stripes every day. We took it slow. Dae went in the direction of studio engineering and production, while I became more immersed in the business side of things.

Tony always deplored being categorized and found any notion of demographics distasteful. He consistently expressed his desire to play to the whole family. In spite of the fact that he was my father, my respect for his artistry would lead the way. His insistence, to this day, on taking musical chances onstage (something he calls "moving the furniture around") keeps his performance relevant and engaging to his audience night after night. He turns a

Danny and Tony Bennett on the red carpet before the "Tony Bennett Celebrates 90: The Best Is Yet to Come" event at Radio City Music Hall, New York, September 15, 2016.

phrase that whispers into the ear of each and every member of the audience as if every word is meant for only them. Experiencing this transcendent quality for myself is what convinced me that he needed only to be exposed, in the right manner, to a broader-aged audience and that they would be transfixed as much as I was by his artistry and the true art of excellence.

What happened after that was decade after decade of breaking all the rules and setting new career benchmarks that redefined the way people listened to music. In fact, Tony heralded in the iPod generation of the nineties with his GRAMMY® Award–winning Album of the Year for his *MTV Unplugged* record, which made it okay for kids to listen to Nirvana and Nine Inch Nails alongside the likes of Tony, Frank, and Billie Holiday. To this day he is not only breaking the rules but, at the age of ninety-two, defying gravity—still at the top of his game and singing better than ever to sold-out audiences across the globe.

My favorite story that Tony loves to tell is when Duke Ellington was told by his record company president that he was going to drop Duke from the label. When Duke asked why, the president said that he wasn't selling records. Duke replied that he was confused, as he thought that he was supposed to make the records and the company was supposed to sell them. This has been my guiding edict for my entire career.

Tony has taught me that great art and music is defined by its ability to arrest one's imagination and keep one suspended in the moment. To feel the love and to cherish every one of those moments. And yes, it took me a long time to understand that's what makes music either good or bad.

I continue to be proud, humbled, and honored to work with my father, a humanitarian and a great artist who will continue to amaze generation after generation from now until the end of time.

And that, my friends, is not my opinion—it's a fact!

—Danny Bennett

> " IN SPITE OF THE FACT THAT HE WAS MY FATHER, MY RESPECT FOR HIS ARTISTRY WOULD LEAD THE WAY. HIS INSISTENCE, TO THIS DAY, ON TAKING MUSICAL CHANCES ONSTAGE (SOMETHING HE CALLS 'MOVING THE FURNITURE AROUND') KEEPS HIS PERFORMANCE RELEVANT AND ENGAGING TO HIS AUDIENCE NIGHT AFTER NIGHT. "

—DANNY BENNETT

introduction

MY FIRST EXPERIENCE OF SEEING TONY BENNETT LIVE IN CONCERT WAS IN DECEMBER 1964, FIFTY-FOUR YEARS AGO, WHEN HE APPEARED FOR A WEEK OF SOLD-OUT CONCERTS AT ONE OF AMERICA'S FINEST SUPPER CLUBS—BLINSTRUB'S VILLAGE AT THE CORNER OF WEST BROADWAY AND D STREET IN SOUTH BOSTON. THE CROWD'S EXCITEMENT AND ANTICIPATION IN BOSTON BEFORE THE SHOW THAT NIGHT WAS THE SAME AS IT HAD BEEN AT THE TIME WHEN TONY APPEARED BEFORE SOLD-OUT AUDIENCES AT CARNEGIE HALL, THE WALDORF, OR THE COPA IN NEW YORK; THE EMPIRE ROOM OR THE PALMER HOUSE IN CHICAGO; THE COCOANUT GROVE OR THE HOLLYWOOD BOWL IN LOS ANGELES; OR CAESAR'S PALACE IN LAS VEGAS. IN BOSTON, IT WAS STANLEY BLINSTRUB'S SUPPER CLUB THAT ATTRACTED A GALAXY OF ENTERTAINMENT ICONS—FRANK SINATRA, JOHNNY MATHIS, SAMMY DAVIS—EVERY TOP-NOTCH ENTERTAINER HAD APPEARED IN THIS LEGENDARY CLUB. JIMMY DURANTE CALLED IT HIS "HOME AWAY FROM HOME."

Tony onstage at the Copacabana, New York, 1966

During the late fall and early winter of 1964, British Invasion bands such as the Beatles, the Kinks, and the Animals, among others, dominated the charts. Yet the week of Tony's engagement in Boston, it seemed every radio station had his latest hit record—"Who Can I Turn To," a Leslie Bricusse–Anthony Newley composition that had been released in November and had quickly charted on *Billboard* magazine's Top 40—on frequent rotation. In fact you could not turn on a radio in America during that time and listen for more than an hour without hearing at least one Tony Bennett record being played. Although I was still attending college at Northeastern University in Boston, I had been a radio host at WCOP-AM for a few years, and Tony's recordings were an essential ingredient in my radio work.

During that show in Boston he earned at least seven standing ovations and had to do two encore numbers before the audience reluctantly allowed him to leave the stage. I'd never seen anything quite like what he did that night. I had been able to make arrangements for a Tony Bennett interview after the show, and when I was escorted to his dressing room, I shook hands with him and then nervously began setting up my Wollensak T-1980 tape recorder on a small table between our two seats. Amazingly Tony was calm and grounded after an emotional evening onstage. I was impressed with how welcoming he was to me—this young radio guy who would probably be asking the same questions Tony had heard during hundreds of interviews, and yet he seemed really pleased to be there. I remember beginning our recording by congratulating him on his memorable performance that evening and then went on to say how much I enjoyed his new *Who Can I Turn To* album.

"Although everyone is playing the title song," I went on, "I've been playing that Cy Coleman–Carolyn Leigh track, "I Walk a Little Faster." That now-famous Tony Bennett radiant smile flashed, and he turned to a lady friend

I had brought backstage with me and said, "Finally, a DJ with ears!" It was an unforgettable evening for me—both the onstage and backstage moments—and subsequently, for over a half-century through my radio work I've had the honor of countless hours of interviews and personal conversations with Tony. I don't think an hour of my more than fifty years of radio work has passed without my programs being enriched by featuring at least one of his unique recordings—so my impression of his place in our history is not only my own opinion but it is very much informed by the feedback I've received from listeners.

Another essential component to my perspective on Tony Bennett's unique career is that I've had the great fortune to witness dozens of his live concerts; each one has been a unique and indelible event. Recently, more than fifty years after that first concert I witnessed in Boston, I was in the audience during one of his shows. Tony began singing the verse to his 1963 hit, "This Is All I Ask." When

he sang "As I approach the prime of my life," there was a soft, knowing chuckle from the audience. When they heard that line from an artist who had his first number-one record when Harry Truman was in the White House, and here, in the twenty-first century, is still totally in command of his gift, they were all thinking, "Tony Bennett, what do you mean, as you APPROACH the prime of your life? You've been IN your prime for over sixty years!" And the coda to that rich experience was at the end when he sang, "And let the music play as long as there's a song to sing / And I will stay younger than spring." The man and song are one. The standing ovation was electrifying, just as it was more than a half-century ago when I first saw him perform.

ABOVE, FROM LEFT TO RIGHT: *Tony during a recording session at CBS 30th Street Studio, 1959; signing autographs at the stage door of the Paramount Theatre, 1951; singing at the Copacabana, 1956—all in New York.*

1

"TOUCHING *the* EARTH *with* LOVE"

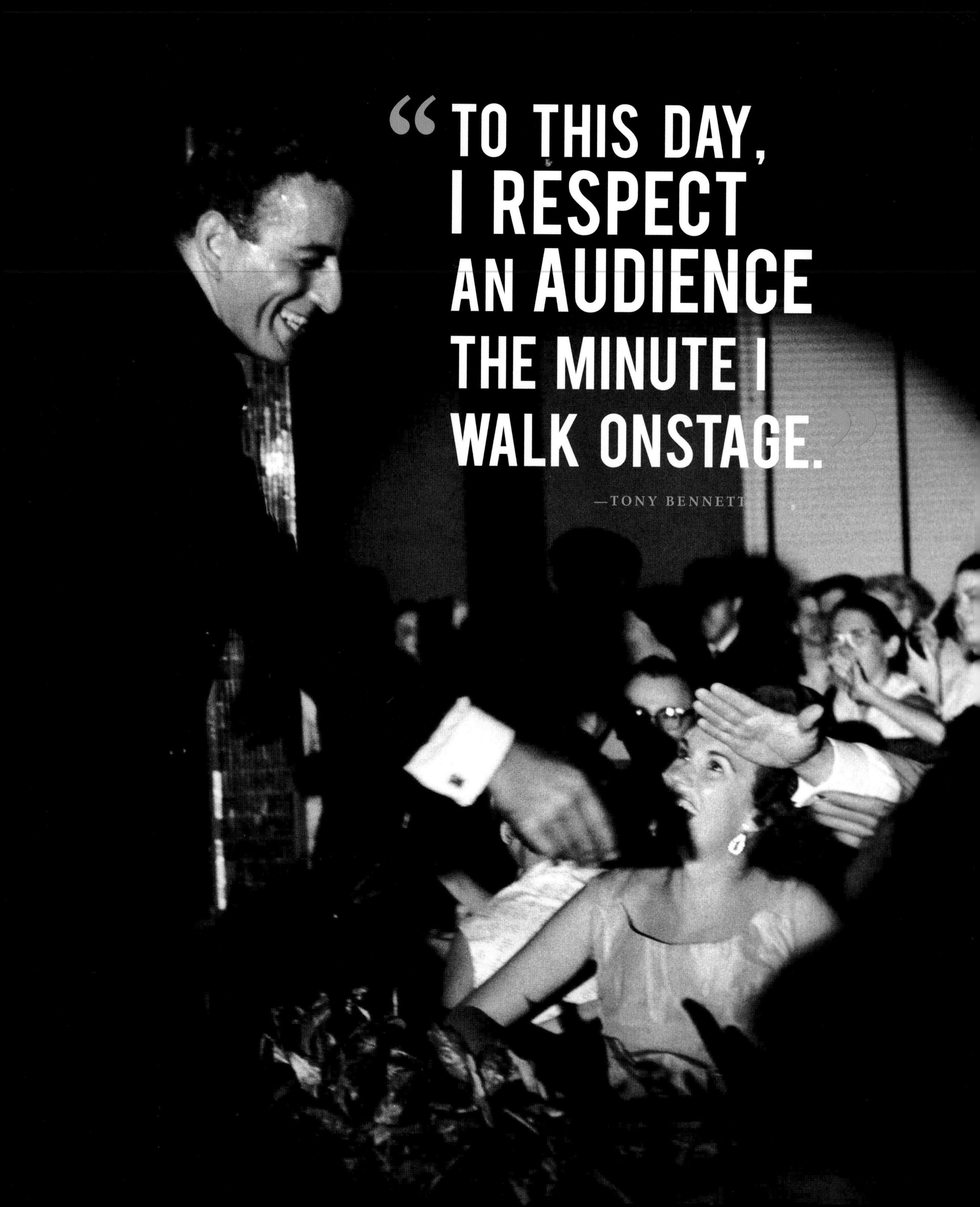

"**TO THIS DAY, I RESPECT AN AUDIENCE THE MINUTE I WALK ONSTAGE.**

—TONY BENNETT

Now seven decades into his career, Tony Bennett still inspires fans all over the world and continues to generate a unique bond with his audiences. The genuine love he radiates onstage and projects back to them has been a consistent part of his journey from the very beginning. I believe part of his unprecedented success and relevance is predicated on his personal character and his authenticity, which he brings with him each time he appears onstage or walks into the recording studio.

Recently Tony told me that some of the most important guidance he received about proper interaction between an artist and an audience took place in the 1950s. As his career began to blossom, he sought advice from someone whose artistry he greatly appreciated, Frank Sinatra. "I loved his music and saw him perform at the Paramount Theatre in New York when I was a teenager," Tony recalled.

I admired his command onstage. I was just becoming widely known when I met him, and I told him that I still had "the jitters" when I was going to go onstage to perform, and that I'd just been given a great professional opportunity: the summer replacement hosting spot for Perry Como's popular television show. And he gave me the best advice that any entertainer or any performer could ever get. He said, "Don't be afraid of the audience. If you like them, they're going to like you. And if you look a little nervous on the camera, they'll sense it. And they'll help you." Imagine that good advice. . . . I never think in terms of I've heard other performers say, "That audience was cold tonight." There's no such thing as a cold audience, only a cold performer.

If you have the spirit, you go out there. The audience senses it right away, and they sit up in their chairs. And they're ready to give you a good reaction to your performance. And it was Sinatra who took a lot of fear out of me about audiences. He taught me to trust them, to stay close to your audience. Show your appreciation, and give the audience the very best performance you can; I always attempt to do that when I walk out on a stage. My concerts are a shared experience. The audience is what inspires my performance.

PREVIOUS PAGES: *Tony Bennett smiles after a performance at the Copacabana, New York, 1967.* OPPOSITE: *Tony shakes hands with audience members at a nightclub, 1957.* ABOVE: *Onstage at the Latin Casino, 1963.*

"[RICHARD] RODGERS LEANED OVER TO ME AND SAID, 'TONY, ALWAYS LISTEN TO THE AUDIENCE....THEY WILL TELL YOU IF YOU'RE DOING IT RIGHT!' HEARING THIS FROM SUCH A 'GIANT' CONFIRMED FOR ME THAT WHEN YOU'RE ON A STAGE, FOCUS ON THE BUSINESS AT HAND."

—TONY BENNETT

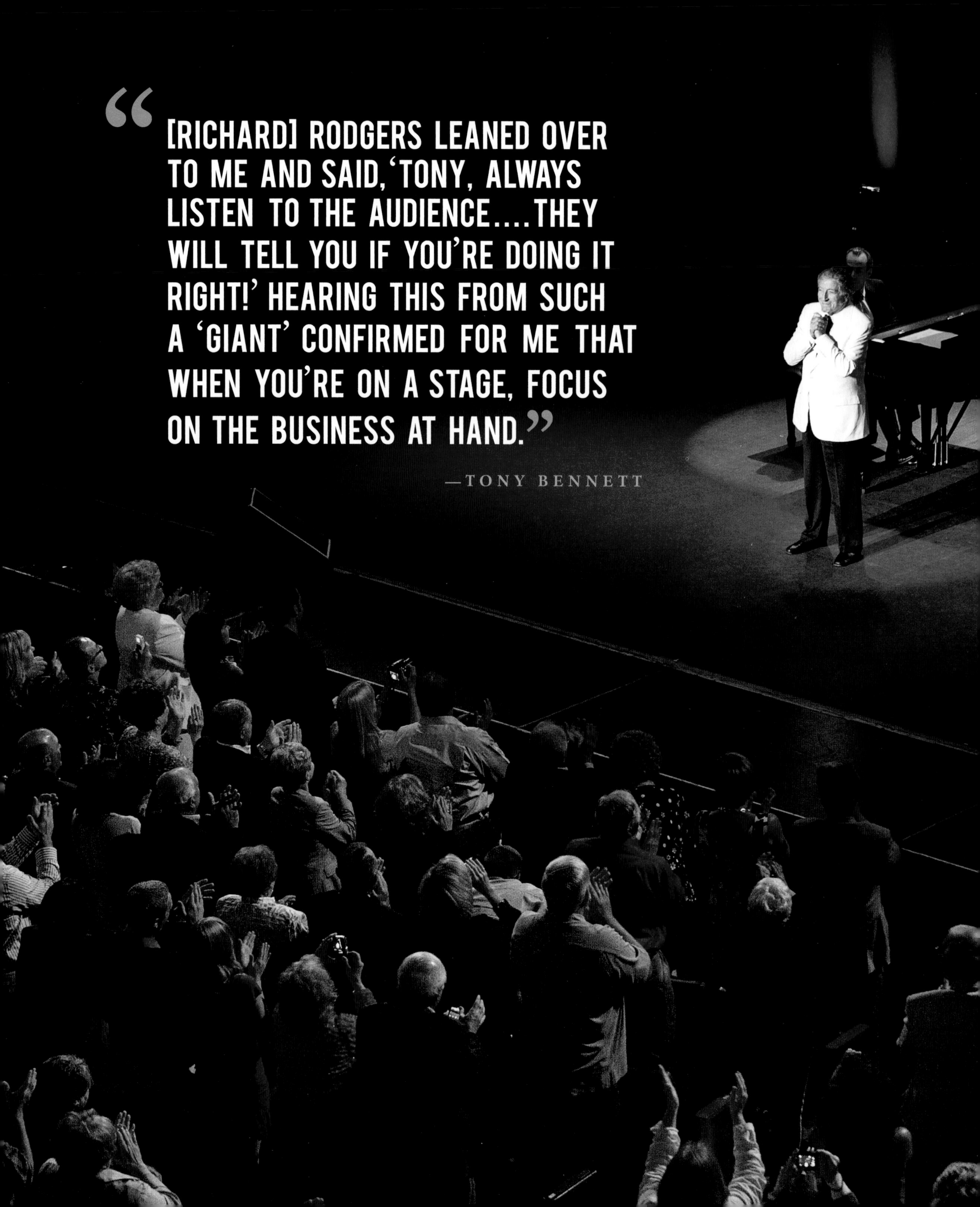

This counsel helped Tony in making a commitment to "stay close to the audience." Years later he told me, "I was on Merv Griffin's television program one day, and the other guest was the marvelous composer Richard Rodgers. When Merv went into a commercial break, Mr. Rodgers leaned over to me and said, 'Tony, always listen to the audience. Don't fixate on what the critics write. Listen closely to the audience. . . . They will tell you if you're doing it right!' Hearing this from such a 'giant' confirmed for me that when you're on a stage focus on the business at hand. . . . Give the audience the best you can!"

The Canadian journalist, music critic, lyricist—and Tony Bennett's friend—Gene Lees—(who wrote the English lyrics for Brazilian composer Antônio Carlos Jobim's "Quiet Nights of Quiet Stars," among other Bennett classics) perhaps captured the essence of this relationship between the artist and the audience when in the early 1970s he recounted this story: "Tony Bennett and I were walking down Seventh Avenue in New York City one day. A workman shoved his face out of a manhole and called 'Hi Tony!' Tony called back with a wave, lighting up like a Christmas tree."

Tony loved the incident, Gene said, and it reveals how Bennett continues to be inspired by his close connection to the audience—a relationship that is still going strong today and has helped make him one of the greatest singers of American popular music.

A special moment between Tony and his audience during a concert at the F.M. Kirby Center in Wilkes-Barre, Pennsylvania, June 2, 2012.

"HOMETOWN, MY TOWN"

Tony is a child of New York City streets; he grew up on them in Astoria, Queens. Anthony Benedetto was born in Astoria on August 3, 1926, to John and Anna Benedetto. He received his early education at the High School of Industrial Arts on Manhattan's Upper East Side and, at home, was exposed to Al Jolson, Bing Crosby, and Enrico Caruso records. After school each day Tony would join his friends in going to hear the big bands performing their matinee concerts (this is when he first saw a live Frank Sinatra–Tommy Dorsey concert at the Paramount Theatre), and then he would visit the Metropolitan Museum of Art, a few blocks from his school, to study and absorb the work of master painters.

OPPOSITE, TOP LEFT: *Tony poses on a chair at age one in Astoria, Queens, 1927.* OPPOSITE, TOP RIGHT: *Tony (front, center), flanked by his sister, Mary Benedetto; father, John Benedetto Sr.; and brother, John Benedetto Jr., 1932.* OPPOSITE, BOTTOM: *Siblings John Jr. (on pony), Mary, and Tony, 1931.* ABOVE: *Tony Bennett at the Triborough Bridge, Astoria, 1944.*

He had to leave New York for the first time in his life when the army called in 1944. Tony shipped overseas and began several years of service with the 255th Infantry Regiment of the 63rd Infantry Division, where he saw action on the front lines. When Germany surrendered, Tony was then assigned to Special Services, the army's entertainment branch. It was a seminal moment in his life in music because he was invited to join the 255th Regiment band, where he got one of his first opportunities to sing for his fellow soldiers. This experience—singing the popular music of the day, songs with great melodies and evocative lyrics like "I'll Be Seeing You," "It Could Happen to You," "Blues in the Night," and "Sentimental Journey"—generated quite an enthusiastic response from the audience.

Seeing how the songs lifted the spirits of those young men and how deeply they were moved was, for Tony, a significant demonstration of the power of music.

That experience really helped Tony to decide to pursue a life in music. He had continued to sketch when he was in the army, but his gratifying musical experiences had fueled his passion for entertaining. When the war ended and he was able to return to his beloved New York in 1946, he chose to attend the American Theatre Wing on his GI Bill of Rights benefits. He applied under the GI bill for study at the American Theatre Wing's professional school, where he studied drama, diction, music theory, and something that continues to influence his singing: the bel canto ("beautiful singing") method of vocal performance, which he studied under a teacher named Pietro D'Andrea. The influence of his vocal teacher was so profound on Tony that he named his first son, born in 1954, after D'Andrea.

ABOVE, LEFT TO RIGHT: *Drawings by Tony Bennett done while he was in France with the 255th Infantry during World War II,* France *and* France Rooftops, *both from 1945; Tony's US Army dog tags.* **OPPOSITE:** *Tony entertaining the troops, 1945 (top); performing with the 255th Regiment band, 1945 (bottom).*

"WHEN I THINK BACK ON THOSE MOMENTS I THINK OF THE RECEPTION WE RECEIVED FROM THOSE WONDERFUL AUDIENCES... YOUNG MEN FAR AWAY FROM HOME AND TO HAVE WITNESSED THE HORROR AND INSANITY OF WAR....IT WAS SO INSPIRING TO BE ABLE TO LIFT THEIR SPIRITS."

—TONY BENNETT

Tony's musical education continued in the clubs of New York, where he and his friends frequented the many clubs located in Midtown along 52nd Street, or "Swing Street," the heart of jazz in New York City. Tony once told me that as a young man he and his friends would get together, and "we would visit as many of the clubs on 52nd Street as possible. We didn't drink; we just listened."

Tony was also studying with vocal coach Mimi Speer, who had a studio on 52nd Street near the Onyx Club just off Sixth Avenue. She would advise him to try not to sound like any other popular male singer but rather to imitate a jazz musician's style. Tony was inspired by saxophonist Stan Getz and pianist Art Tatum as he developed his singing style. "I loved the honey sound that Stan was able to create when he played; it was a full and warm sound. And I was so impressed at the way Art Tatum would make a production out of the song he was playing. He would move in and out of the melody, and this created a presentation that kept the listener engaged. Their influence helped shaped me. . . . What I learned from listening to them has been my approach to singing."

> **" EVEN TODAY IT SEEMS LIKE A DREAM TO ME—IN ONE NIGHT TO SEE BILLIE HOLIDAY, ERROLL GARNER, MILES DAVIS, DIZZY GILLESPIE, OR LOUIS ARMSTRONG PLAYING AT THE PEAK OF THEIR CAREERS....WE STAYED FOR AS LONG AS WE COULD, AND I REMEMBER MANY TIMES LEAVING WHEN THE SUN WAS ALREADY UP. WE ALL THOUGHT AND HOPED THAT IT WOULD LAST FOREVER. "**
>
> —TONY BENNETT

The neon lights of the clubs of 52nd Street—Swing Street—in New York City, 1948.

Tony's journey to fame began in the late 1940s, after his stint with the American Theatre Wing. In November 1949, the legendary Pearl Bailey came into Tony's life when she heard him sing at the Greenwich Village Inn in New York City, where she was planning to stage a revue. Bailey instantly recognized his talent and put him in the show. She then invited Bob Hope to come see for himself the young singer Joe Bari (Tony's original stage name) she'd been telling Hope about. Hope was so impressed he made the young man a part of his Paramount Theatre show and changed Anthony Benedetto's stage name from Joe Bari to Tony Bennett. It was about this time that Pearl Bailey also warned Tony to avoid a common malady that can befall entertainers: "Beware of a lethal disease that can affect people in show business," she advised, "It's called 'helium of the brain'! Never stop learning to grow as an artist, and always respect the audience and give it all to them."

The music Tony first heard in those early days of living, growing, and learning in New York City, and the energy he continues to receive from living there, is one of the constants in his life. Even today he refuses to isolate himself from his audience, no matter how huge the crowd. The recognition Tony receives from the general public as he walks down the streets, visits Central Park with his wife, Susan, or ducks into a Manhattan coffeehouse with his daughter Johanna—these personal encounters—seemingly means more to Tony than all the admiration of the famous who are his friends. Not long ago, Tony told me how gratifying it was to hear from people about the significance his music has played in their lives. "I meet many people who stop and say, 'Thank you, Tony, for the music. I've been listening to you through the years, and your records are like a soundtrack to my life.' How rewarding this is to hear . . . to know that what you've been attempting to do with music— to make recordings of only the very best American songs surrounded by superb musicians—has had such a positive impact on people's lives."

OPPOSITE: *Tony Bennett is approached by autograph seekers as he leaves a performance on October 4, 1951.* ABOVE: *Tony surprises an excited crowd while walking through Central Park after a painting session, New York, November 2015.*

> **"AS A CHILD GROWING UP IN ASTORIA, I WOULD LOOK ACROSS THE RIVER AND GAZE AT THE SKYSCRAPERS IN MANHATTAN AND BE IN AWE OF THEIR MAJESTY. I JUST NEVER COULD HAVE IMAGINED THAT THE EMPIRE STATE BUILDING WOULD BE A PART OF MY BIRTHDAY CELEBRATION."**

OPPOSITE: *Lady Gaga, Stevie Wonder, and Paul McCartney were among the friends and family celebrating Tony's ninetieth birthday at the Rainbow Room in New York City, August 3, 2016.*

"THE GOOD LIFE"

My hope is that a hundred or so years from now some astute historian or musicologist—after discovering the treasure trove of Tony Bennett's recorded artistry and becoming aware of the longevity of his career in popular music and jazz—will be curious about the man behind the recordings and they will find this book. They may wonder just how Mr. Bennett, after achieving his first successes as a recording artist in the midpart of the twentieth century, endured as a relevant artist through the innumerable shifts in taste and technology that have occurred in the twenty-first century. Most human beings peak at a certain point in life, and then their powers begin to diminish. Tony's great ambition at ninety, was, as he often stated, "to get better and better. To keep growing and to keep creating." As Tony Bennett celebrated his ninetieth birthday year in 2016, how did he sound and what level of physical energy did he bring to his performance? Was he still able to dazzle and surprise audiences? Did he demonstrate onstage that he was still "a work in progress"?

To give that researcher some insight of what the world witnessed in 2016, I will attempt a brief recapitulation of Tony's professional life in his ninetieth year. This fact in itself is astounding. I am recapping here the story of a singer not when he was twenty or thirty-five, which you might consider peak years, but by recounting just a few examples of events that occurred in an unprecedented year in the artist's life when he was ninety!

Early in 2016, on February 15 at the 58th Annual GRAMMY Awards at the Staples Center in Los Angeles, Tony Bennett won his eighteenth GRAMMY (he had won his first two at the 5th Annual GRAMMYs in 1963) for a critically acclaimed CD tribute to the composer many feel is at the top of that pantheon of American Songbook music composers: Jerome Kern. On September 23, 2015, in the *New York Times* review of *The Silver Lining: The Songs of Jerome Kern*, featuring pianist Bill Charlap collaborating with Tony Bennett, critic Nate Chinen observed that, "'On Pick Yourself Up,' [Tony] injects Dorothy Fields's pep-talk lyrics with special gusto. . . . He radiates pluck and purpose, a conviction that what matters is the drive to keep going. It's not a message to take lightly now, if indeed it ever was."

Following the GRAMMYs, Tony performed almost thirty concerts around the world through the spring and summer of 2016, pausing on the evening of August 3 to celebrate his ninetieth birthday at a grand party held at the iconic Rainbow Room at Rockefeller Center in New York. With the encouragement of musical icon Lady Gaga, Mayor Bill de Blasio had proclaimed it "Tony Bennett Day" in New York. Tony was surrounded by his loving family and many friends from the worlds of entertainment, politics, and art, including New York governor Andrew Cuomo, director Martin Scorsese, Lady Gaga, and musical icons Harry Belafonte, Paul McCartney, and Stevie Wonder.

At one point in the evening, Tony's son Danny, who has been his father's manager for over thirty years and had produced this celebration, invited Tony and Lady Gaga to the stage. He directed them to press a nearby button, which resulted in the Empire State Building lighting up in the colors of the American and Italian flags in Tony's honor.

Tony later told me what a thrill that night was:

As a child growing up in Astoria, I would look across the river and gaze at the skyscrapers in Manhattan and be in awe of their majesty. I just never could have imagined that the Empire State Building, the most visible building at that time, would be a part of my birthday celebration. My relatives were immigrants to this country and loved the opportunities it gave them, and so to see the colors of both America and Italy was truly wonderful. I thought in that moment how much my parents and family loved their adopted country and how much I gained by being raised in such a wonderful city like New York. I was only five years old in 1931, when President Hoover turned on those lights to officially open the building! And then eighty-five years later in my life, this magical evening!

* * *

ABOVE: *Lady Gaga sings to Tony Bennett in celebration of his birthday at the Rainbow Room, August 3, 2016.*

A little over two weeks after celebrating his August 3 birthday at home, part two of a grand coast-to-coast celebration began with Tony and his family traveling to San Francisco. Tony Bennett's artistry and the beautiful city of San Francisco are forever intertwined. It is widely acknowledged by many people who live in that lovely city that partly because of Tony Bennett's 1962 recording of "I Left My Heart in San Francisco," their city has become a worldwide destination for millions. This is in large measure because of the images Bennett's signature song has evoked in the minds of listeners, Tony had introduced his version of the song—composed in 1953 by George Cory with lyrics by Douglass Cross—in December 1961 at an engagement in that city at the Fairmont Hotel's Venetian Room; then, about three weeks later, on January 23, 1962, in New York City, he recorded what has now become San Francisco's anthem.

The Golden Gate Bridge shrouded in fog on the I Left My Heart In San Francisco *album cover, released in 1962.*

BELOW: *A sketch of the Golden Gate Bridge by Tony Bennett.*

I once mentioned to Tony that up until his 1962 recording of the song, if you had asked most people the first thing that came to mind when they thought of San Francisco, many of them would have said "earthquake," in reference to the deadly and tragic event that nearly destroyed the city in April 1906. Tony projected a new picture of the city to a worldwide audience and helped change its image to one of romance and enduring beauty.

Tony responded with a chuckle:

> I find it humorous when someone comes up to me and says, "Don't you get tired of singing 'I Left My Heart in San Francisco'?" And I say, no because it's the most magnificent city. The natural beauty, the rich culture, and the people. The citizens of San Francisco, for the last sixty years, have been so wonderful to me. I can't tell you how I feel about that place. Whenever my wife, Susan—who grew up in the Bay Area—and I are in San Francisco, I feel like royalty. Really, the citizens are so kind, that's the way they treat us. . . . I love visiting and performing there.

The song's importance as part America's cultural legacy was acknowledged in March 2018, fifty-six years after the recording was first released, when Librarian of Congress Carla Hayden included the record as part of the newest recordings to be added to the National Recording Registry of the Library of Congress. In announcing the distinction, Dr. Hayden said of Tony's recording and the other historical audio treasures deemed worthy of the library's preservation: "The unique trinity of historic, cultural, and aesthetic significance reflected in the National Recording Registry each year is an opportunity for reflection on landmark moments, diverse cultures, and shared memories—all reflected in our recorded soundscape."

The backstory to how the song ended up in Tony Bennett's hands is worthy of a movie. Tony Bennett and Ralph Sharon, Tony's music director, were always on the lookout for new songs written by the next generation of compos-

ers. Ralph would vet any potential song material that was sent their way to see if it had potential before he reviewed the material with Tony. For over two decades, one of the highlights of the summer season on Cape Cod was the annual Tony Bennett concert at the Cape Cod Melody Tent in Hyannis, Massachusetts, founded by stage legend Gertrude Lawrence in 1950. Without fail every year, a month or so before Tony would arrive, I would receive in the mail sheet music for songs written by various amateur songwriters in the area who would implore me to get their songs into Tony's hands to see if he might be interested in recording them. Because of their passion and their loyalty as listeners, I would promise them that while I couldn't hand their efforts over directly to Tony, I would pass them to his music director. The first time I did this, Ralph could not have been kinder or more understanding. He promised me that he would review the songs at some point, and if there was anything of interest in what I had given him, he had the contact information of the songwriters.

On one such occasion in 1984, as Ralph put the manuscripts into his carrying case, he said to me, "Well, you never know. This is how 'San Francisco' came to be." He then elaborated, telling me that in the early 1950s, after he moved from London to New York, he met two amateur songwriters, Douglass Cross and George Cory. They had grown up in the San Francisco area, served in World War II, and then, as aspiring songwriters, they moved to New York hoping to be discovered as composers. Ralph explained:

> I knew from comments they'd made that they didn't like New York City because they missed the Bay Area so much. One day, after I had joined Tony Bennett as his music director, they handed me a song called "I Left My Heart in San Francisco," and I told them at some point I would look at it. When I got home and unpacked I just put the song in a drawer in my dresser and forgot about it.

Tony waves from a cable car in San Francisco, 1975.

Maybe it was a year later, we were going on a Southwest/West concert tour. I was packing, and while going through a drawer for some shirts, there was the Cross/Cory song "I Left My Heart in San Francisco." Now, the title jumped of the page, because I knew that one of the engagements we were looking forward to a week in late December was the Venetian Room at the Fairmount Hotel, on Nob Hill in San Francisco.

As we got closer to San Francisco, I ran down the song for Tony to get his reaction, and he thought it would be perfect to include in the Fairmount series.

On December 22, 1961, at the first Tony Bennett concert of a series promoted by the hotel as the "Happy New Year Concerts," which would run through January 17, 1962, Tony sang the song; it was met with a standing ovation. From all reports, the warmth and authenticity Tony brought to the first performance of the song connected deeply with the residents of the city who attended the concert.

Less than a week after the Fairmont engagement, Ralph and Tony were scheduled to go into the CBS 30th Street Studios—the "Church"—in New York on Monday, January 23, 1962, to record a new Broadway song called "Once Upon a Time."

"I had heard the song somewhere in that time frame." Tony said, "It was included in the score of a new Broadway show called *All American*, which starred Ray Bolger. The music, written by Charles Strouse, was very nice but I really connected with the Lee Adams lyric. We had that great team all set for the session at Columbia, with Marty Manning, who wrote the arrangement and Frank Laico, who was doing the engineer session. I was really looking forward to recording it."

Ralph had told me that both he and Tony were very pleased at the reception they recently received for "I Left My Heart in San Francisco" but both felt that it was perhaps because he was singing the song before a "hometown" audience.

"But one night after one of the concerts, the local Columbia Records promoter visited us in the green room and urged us to put the song on a record. He guaranteed that it would be a hit at least in that city."

On January 23, 1962, when Tony and Ralph went into the recording studio, Tony mentioned to Mitch Miller—the A&R (Artists and Repertoire) man at the session—what the Columbia Records promotional representative had said about "I Left My Heart."

Miller said: "Well, you know if you want to do that, throw it in, but the A-side [code for 'this is the one we want you to play'] of the promotional 45 would be 'Once Upon a

Time.' The B-side [code for 'we needed something for the other side of the record'] could be 'I Left My Heart in San Francisco.'"

At that time in radio, there were some "rebel" air personalities who didn't like be told by record companies "what they should play," and one of those deejays, when auditioning the record, found the B-side to be a *very* good listening experience and played it on air—this resulted in their phones ringing with requests from listeners to play it again. Before long, the word went out to other stations across the country, and they started playing the B-side as well, producing the same results with their listeners. Within a very short period of time, "I Left My Heart in San Francisco" was embraced by the American public. The strong worldwide reaction to Tony Bennett's performance of the song was his musical passport, gaining him international recognition and fame.

Less than six months after the record's release, Tony's performance of the song at his acclaimed Carnegie Hall concert of June 9, 1962, was received with what Ralph Sharon described as a "thunderous ovation." The entire two-hour show turned out to be a historical performance. Directed by Arthur Penn and Gene Saks, the concert was released on two albums in late July 1962. It was a stunning musical summation of Tony Bennett's life as a singer/performer at thirty-six years old.

"Ralph and I put everything into that night" Tony told me, "and I was so pleased that Goddard Lieberson [president] of Columbia suggested that we record the concert. Engineer Frank Laico again that evening did a masterful job I think, of capturing the great acoustics of the hall and of the excitement coming from that sold-out audience. I got my friend Arthur Penn to help me stage the concert and then Gene Saks brought his Broadway directing experience to us. Ralph and I put together a group of very gifted players, people like Eddie Costa, Kenny Burrell, Candido Camero, Joe Soldo, Mel Davis, and Al Cohn. Their playing and that audience reaction was such an inspiration to me that night."

Tony Bennett's drawing of San Francisco's Chinatown.

On the 1997 two-CD release of the entire night's performance, the company included the Ralph Sharon liner notes from the original 1962 LP release. Ralph noted that the collective group, the audience assembled at Carnegie Hall that evening (which included composer Harold Arlen and the technical engineers), witnessed Tony Bennett "meet his greatest challenge and he came through like the champion he is. Listeners will hear the magic combination of Tony singing at top of his form and giving a masterly performance, an orchestra complementing him splendidly throughout, the perfect acoustics of the famous old hall lending themselves to the proceedings and finally the audience themselves, who were with Tony Bennett all the way!"

Over the course of the second half of the twentieth century, "I Left My Heart in San Francisco" continued to be recognized: In 1962, "I Left My Heart in San Francisco" was included in the Song of the Century list by the Recording Industry Association of America, the National Endowment for the Arts, and Scholastic. At the 5th Annual GRAMMY Awards in May 1963, the song was named Record of the Year, and Tony won Best Solo Vocal Performance, Male; Marty Manning earned a GRAMMY for Best Background Arrangement. In 1994, the recording was inducted into the GRAMMY Hall of Fame, and in 2003 earned the Towering Song Award from the Songwriters Hall of Fame. All

Tony's 1963 GRAMMY for Best Solo Performance, Male, for "I Left My Heart in San Francisco."

of this, and so much more, the result of 2 minutes and 51 seconds of excellence captured in the "Church" on January 23, 1962.

I once remarked to Tony that "I Left My Heart in San Francisco" seems to have the same universal appeal as Bing Crosby's recording of Irving Berlin's "White Christmas" because, like the Christmas classic, "I Left My Heart" is about a man who "misses home," just as Douglass Cross and George Cory had. When I first visited the city, and on a foggy, misty morning took a cable car from Nob Hill to the Terminal Building and walked out on the piers, it was like being in heaven, and I finally understood what Tony meant when he sang the song.

The song was also the inspiration for a project begun in 2004, "Hearts in San Francisco," which benefits the San Francisco General Hospital. Each year, artists contribute paintings that are installed and displayed throughout the city; the choice of the "hearts" theme was inspired by Tony Bennett's iconic recording. His "heart painting" is displayed in the city's Union Square section, and I've never passed it without seeing groups in front the painting taking selfies!

The city has never stopped saying "thank you" to Tony, and his love for the city and its people has deepened over the last almost sixty years. With the support of San Francisco officials and residents of the city, Mayor Ed Lee (who sadly died in December 2017) declared Friday, August 19, 2016, "Tony Bennett Day." It appeared that the whole city turned out at noon to gather on Nob Hill in front of the Fairmont Hotel for the unveiling of San Francisco sculptor Bruce Leslie Wolfe's eight-foot-tall bronze statue of Tony. The statue was the culmination of a major initiative by the city's chief of protocol, Charlotte Mailliard Shultz, to honor a favorite son of the city.

At noon, the carillon atop Grace Cathedral located across from the Fairmont played "I Left My Heart in San Francisco." Mayor Lee declared, as he presented Tony with keys to the city, "Tony Bennett, you've helped us share the magic of San Francisco around the world." Former mayor

Willie Brown spoke for everyone in attendance when he declared, "Tony Bennett is an adopted son of our city!"

Senator Barbara Boxer spoke, as did Representative Nancy Pelosi. Chief of Protocol Shultz told me later that day that the song "just made our city so romantic. It captures why we love calling San Francisco our home. And when people around the world hear it, they want to visit and see [this place] for themselves . . . When the cable cars broke down and were closed down for two years and we brought them back, he came to assist us. When we had the earthquake and we put the Bay Bridge back together, he came. He's always here for us, so we thought, 'What can we do for him?' And we thought of the statue."

San Francisco Bay Area sculptor Bruce Leslie Wolfe began creating his wonderful likeness of Tony in 2016. I met Wolfe at the dedication ceremony, and he mentioned that he had the great pleasure of having the singer sit with him for three days while the sculptor began his work. Wolfe said it was both enjoyable and motivational to have Tony's company; they listened to music and had great conversations about art. Wolfe was quite touched that Bennett produced a sketch of him, which he presented to the sculptor on the last day of their sessions. "Tony Bennett is probably the best vocal singer that I've ever heard. He can do anything with words," Wolfe said.

The dedication program on Nob Hill featured music from the SFJAZZ High School All Stars Combo and a beautiful version of "I Left My Heart in San Francisco" sung by the San Francisco Boys and Girls Chorus. With their voices, the song sounded like a hymn, and Tony was very moved as he spoke to the audience: "I can't get over what just happened. That's the most beautiful statue. It will live in my heart forever. Thank you for being so wonderful to me. I'll never forget this day."

The program ended with San Francisco Giants CEO Larry Baer reminding everyone that "Tony Bennett Day" had only just begun, with the festivities to be continued at AT&T Park that evening. The Giants, during their game with the New York Mets, would honor Bennett in a pregame ceremony and throughout the game. Baer said, "Opening day in 1993—who was there to sing . . . when the Giants were saved? Tony Bennett at Candlestick Park. . . . Tony, you're San Francisco royalty. We look forward tonight at the ballpark where we will have a small group of 41,000 people singing 'Happy Birthday' to you!"

An hour later when Tony arrived at the park and was escorted to home plate, there, ready to present him with a Giants jacket, was Baseball Hall of Fame player Willie Mays, who spent twenty-two years playing for the Giants— from 1951 to 1957 in New York and from 1958 to 1972 in San Francisco.

Tony wanted to give back something to the city, so the next night he starred in a gala dinner and concert at the Fairmont that benefited the Tony Bennett Fund for Emergency Pediatric Care at Zuckerberg San Francisco General Hospital.

* * *

OPPOSITE: *Tony Bennett gives a thumbs-up as members of the San Francisco Boys and Girls Chorus and city and state chief of protocol Charlotte Shultz, left, look on, after Tony's statue by Bruce Leslie Wolfe was unveiled outside the Fairmont Hotel atop Nob Hill, August 19, 2016.*

RIGHT: *Former San Francisco Giants legend Willie Mays presents Tony Bennett with a Giants jacket and signed baseball in honor of Tony's ninetieth birthday, prior to the start of the game against the New York Mets at AT&T Park in San Francisco, August 19, 2016.*

BACK EAST, TONY'S NINETIETH BIRTHDAY also inspired a second New York City celebration: a sold-out Radio City Music Hall concert held on September 15, "Tony Bennett Celebrates 90: The Best Is Yet to Come." As Tony and his wife, Susan, quietly entered the hall, some students from the Frank Sinatra School of the Arts, founded by Tony and Susan in 2001, saw them heading to their seats and started applauding. The rest of the five thousand people in the audience quickly saw what was happening and spontaneously rose to their feet and joined the students in the applause, and everyone began singing "Happy Birthday" to Tony. And this was just for walking into the theater! The show, again produced with great love and creativity by Tony's son and manager Danny, featured a galaxy of entertainers including Alec Baldwin, Lady Gaga, Elton John, Bob Dylan, Wynton Marsalis, Stevie Wonder, Billy Joel, k.d. lang, Diana Krall, Andrea Bocelli and the children of the Voices of Haiti Choir, Leslie Odom Jr., and Michael Bublé. This extraordinary evening, which included a Tony Bennett concert segment, was recorded and shown as a two-hour NBC-TV special on December 20, which would be nominated for two Emmys, and the soundtrack would win a GRAMMY in 2018.

"I COULD HAVE RETIRED SIXTEEN YEARS AGO, BUT I JUST LOVE WHAT I'M DOING."

—TONY BENNETT

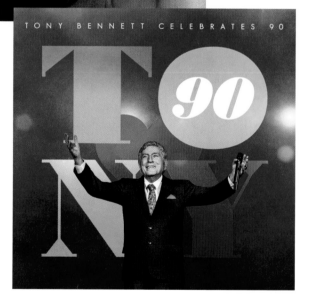

TOP TO BOTTOM: *Tony joins the performers onstage for a birthday serenade at the "Tony Bennett Celebrates 90: The Best Is Yet to Come" concert at Radio City Music Hall, September 15, 2016; Tony Bennett and Lady Gaga at the concert; the cover to the soundtrack of the birthday event, which won the 2018 GRAMMY for Best Traditional Pop Vocal Album.* OPPOSITE: *Tony and his wife, Susan, pose with the proud class of 2011, graduating from the Frank Sinatra School of Arts in Astoria, which was founded by the Bennetts in 2001.*

"I'VE COME HOME AGAIN"

Perhaps one of the highlights of the year for Tony and his wife, Susan, took place on December 1, 2016, when the Frank Sinatra School of Arts in Astoria honored the renowned school's founders. The school epitomizes Tony's lifelong commitment to the arts and the place they should occupy in our nation. In addition to creating the school and then raising the funds to build the facility, back in 1999 Tony and Susan had established Exploring the Arts, a foundation for arts education that assists arts programs in dozens of public high schools. Principal Donna Finn and Chancellor Carmen Farina spoke that evening about the enduring thanks the city of New York has for the vision and leadership Tony and Susan have contributed in establishing the school and the foundation.

Also speaking that evening was an important early supporter of the concept of the school and someone who remembered seeing teenage Tony Bennett sing, former City Council speaker, Peter Vallone Sr. As a fourteen-year-old, Tony was friendly with Vallone's cousins and performed with them in their basement when Peter was six. Peter's father, Charles, a classically trained musician, was so impressed with Tony's singing that he later got him a date to sing for a big social club in Astoria. Peter remembered the standing ovation Anthony Benedetto received that evening and how he captured the audience's attention with his talent.

Introducing Tony and Susan to the auditorium stage, Mr. Vallone noted that the auditorium was designed by Tony Bennett and was probably acoustically second only to Carnegie Hall. Tony reminded me, one day when we were talking, of the great effort and love he and Susan put into building the school and that every day he was inspired by the accomplishment:

> About 97 percent graduate, and 97 percent go to college. It's a very successful school, and it's so spirited. . . . Our funding has helped to create performing arts programs in numerous public schools in New York City

and Los Angeles. And we're counting on and hoping that in every state there will be a strong and vital performing arts agenda. Our belief is that, if the arts flourish in every public school in the United States, we could have more artists than any other country in the world. Think of how much stronger we'll become as a society, because artists focus on truth and beauty. It'll affect everybody, including politicians and corporate executives.

*   *   *

ON THE EVE OF HIS NINETY-FIRST BIRTHDAY—after returning from a triumphal spring tour of Europe, followed by two sold-out concerts at the Hollywood Bowl—Tony Bennett returned to San Francisco. This time, he delighted audiences who attended his two concerts at Davis Symphony Hall, where he performed with the San Francisco Symphony Orchestra. Tony had come full circle in his ninetieth year, performing coast to coast and around the world, doing what has inspired generations for seven decades. Through his singing and painting he has always been committed to attempting to raise the human spirit, to inspire audiences, and to encourage love and harmony. As he recently told me, "I've been so blessed throughout my life to have people who encouraged me to be the best I could be—to stay with the best songs . . . to stay with quality. The thing that lasts is quality, and it never goes out of style. And I've been fortunate to live long enough to have it pay off for me because people adore the music that I sing, and it's been worth the whole trip."

My first Tony Bennett concert was the best concert I never saw.

Back in the early 1960s, when I was growing up in Hot Springs, Arkansas, Tony came to give a show at one of the local clubs in my hometown. At the time, Tony was already a big star with a decade's worth of hits under his belt, and I was just a teenager, midway through high school, with an outsized love of music, hoping to hear him play. In those days, however, Hot Springs was a big, brash place with all the excitement and notoriety of a town that, for several years, had the largest illegal gambling operation in the United States—and a firm stance on keeping underage kids like me out of clubs like the Vapors, where Tony was slated to play.

Not wanting to miss hearing the songs I loved sung by a singer I admired, I'll confess to spending a good part of the evening in front of the Vapors trying to talk my way into Tony's performance. Try as I might, no amount of cajoling was able to get me past the front door, and I never was able to get into that show. I only recently learned that Ralph Sharon, Tony's longtime pianist, showed him "I Left My Heart in San Francisco" for the first time that night after their show, and even though I'm sorry I wasn't there, I'll always be proud that Tony debuted his signature song in my hometown.

Thankfully, I've had better luck getting into Tony's shows in the years since, and it's been a privilege to hear him perform so many times over the course of his long career. Everyone knows that Tony is a gifted artist, but what makes Tony truly special is not the greatness of his talent or the longevity of his career, but the size of his heart. Throughout his life, he has never lost sight of the power of giving back—and whether serving in the army or sharing his love of the arts with students across the country through his Exploring the Arts Foundation, Tony's life can be measured not just in best-selling albums, but in lives made better by his selflessness.

I will always be personally grateful to Tony for performing at my first inaugural and for lending his talents, time and again, to support the work of the Clinton Foundation. And we should all be grateful that, for more than sixty years, Tony has brought his love of American song to adoring fans around the world. With his remarkable voice and generous spirit, it's no wonder they continue to return that love in equal measure.

I've always said that Tony has perfect pitch both in music and in life, and it's as true today as it was in Hot Springs more than 50 years ago. . . . Happy Birthday, Tony, and thank you for your songs, for your friendship, and for setting an example of a life well-lived.

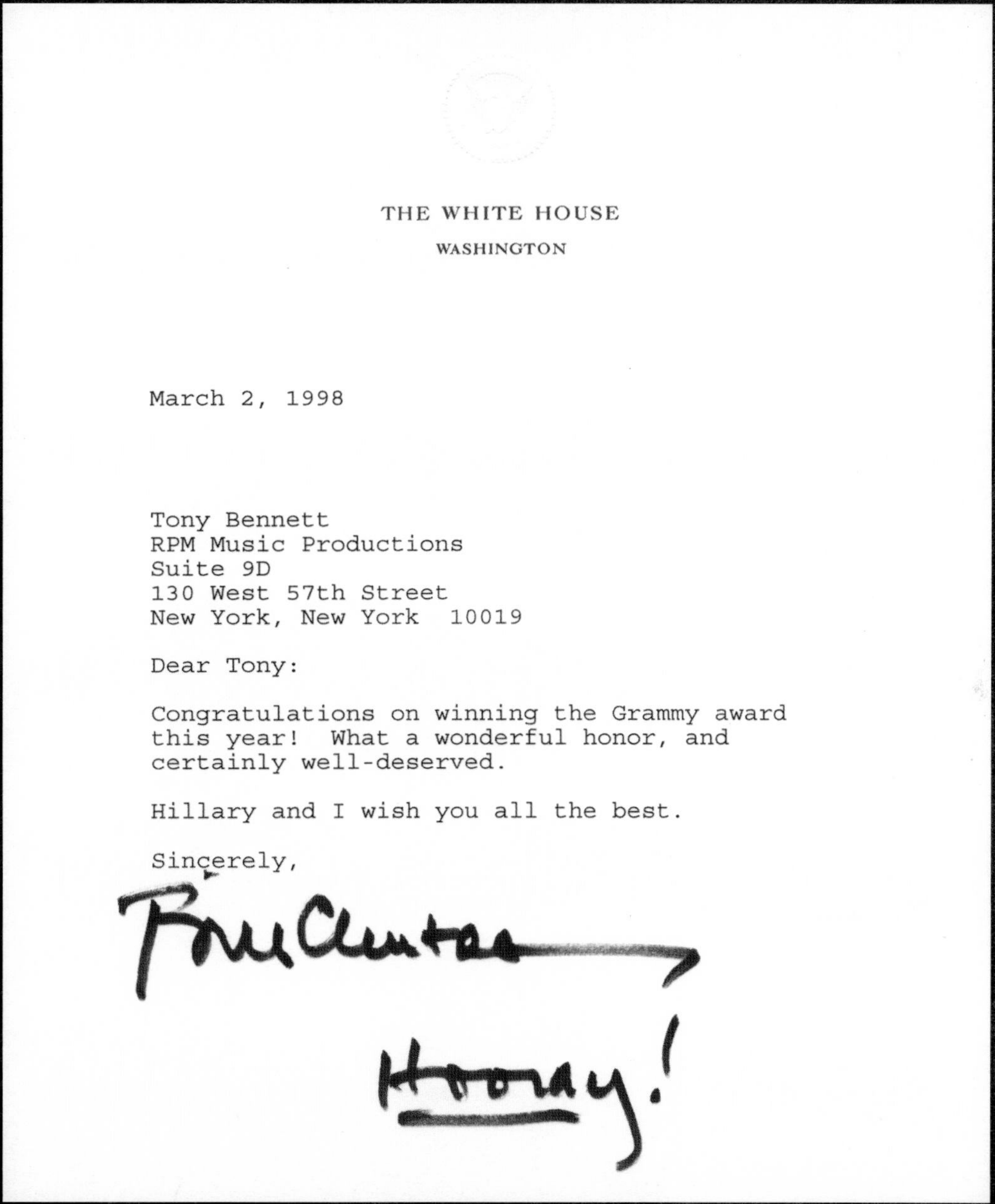

THE WHITE HOUSE
WASHINGTON

March 2, 1998

Tony Bennett
RPM Music Productions
Suite 9D
130 West 57th Street
New York, New York 10019

Dear Tony:

Congratulations on winning the Grammy award
this year! What a wonderful honor, and
certainly well-deserved.

Hillary and I wish you all the best.

Sincerely,

Bill Clinton

Hooray!

ABOVE: *A letter from President Clinton congratulating Tony on his* GRAMMY *win in 1998 (Best Traditional Pop Vocal Performance, for* Tony Bennett on Holiday **OPPOSITE**: *President Bill Clinton and Tony Bennett speak during the Clinton Global Initiative 2015 Global Citizen Awards at the Sheraton Times Square hotel, New York, September 27, 2015.*

2
PORTRAIT *of the* ARTIST: ASTORIA

"I'VE COME HOME AGAIN / TO WHERE IT ALL BEGAN."

—"I'VE COME HOME AGAIN,"
WRITTEN FOR TONY BENNETT BY
CHARLES DEFOREST, 1989

The foundation for Tony Bennett's life's work—the commitment to express what it means to be alive through music and painting—was established during his childhood in a loving and supportive family home.

One evening in September 1998, when Tony and I were deep into a phone call that had been mostly focused on his childhood, he stopped in midsentence and with great emotion told me,

"I think I just identified the moment when I decided that I must do something significant with my life. After my dad died, my mother not only had to work long hours daily as a seamstress at a shop in the Garment District [in New York City], she then would work at home late into the night hemming dresses for neighborhood customers, which allowed her to earn extra money to help raise her three children. I could never completely fall asleep because on occasion, as she was working, she would accidentally stab a finger with one of the long sharp needles she had to work with and I could hear her painful reaction. It's so clear to me now that as I was lying there I would say to myself 'I've got to do something with my life that will allow me to take mom away from this. . . . I've got to be successful enough to be able to make her life better.'"

I replied, "And so the whole premise of all the success you've earned over many decades, the core value of what motivated you . . . was love!"

During the three decades of conversations I've had with Tony, I've learned that he does not spend too much time in the past but that he is always thinking about and planning the next project: the next album, tomorrow night's concert, or a new painting. However, I've also been impressed with the many times he acknowledged his gratitude to his family for their encouragement of his boyhood passions to paint and sing.

PREVIOUS PAGES: *Tony Bennett performing in 1957*
OPPOSITE: *Tony and his mother, Anna, 1944.* ABOVE: *Tony's parents, Anna and John Benedetto, 1930s.*

As a young boy, Tony was first inspired by music because of his dad's fine singing voice. His father, John, who sadly died of congestive heart failure when Tony was ten, was viewed by his relatives and friends as having a highly developed sense of justice. Whenever a problem came up, Tony's dad would be summoned to arbitrate because of his reputation for fairness.

Tony remembers a story his mother told him about his dad discovering a robber in the family grocery store: "My mother told me that the police were summoned, and when they arrived and were about to arrest the thief, my dad asked the man why he was committing a robbery. The man answered, 'I have no job, and my family is hungry.' My father's response was to offer the man a job in the store!

What a strong lesson of compassion and kindness for a young boy to learn from his father."

Tony and his older siblings, John Jr. and Mary, also learned from their father to appreciate both painting and classic novels. John Sr. often read to his children, exposing them to the philosophy of authors such as Fyodor Dostoevsky, Thomas Mann, and Charles Dickens. His father also inspired in young Anthony a love of singing.

> My dad had a beautiful singing voice. When we were kids, my brother, John, and I would just sit and listen when our father would spontaneously begin to sing in the living room or when he would entertain relatives who gathered together in our home. I was as lost as a child when he died. Talking with you about him now, I just remembered a moment with my father that has never been far from my thinking about him. One afternoon, when I was about nine, I was in the living room by myself drawing a picture with a crayon set I had. My father was sick and had been bedridden in his room. Suddenly I looked up, and there was my father coming toward me. He moved very slowly and must have had to summon all his energy to get out of bed to visit with me. He didn't say a word. He just came to me and hugged me. He squeezed me so tightly I can feel it even now as I speak to you. I now think he did that to try and communicate to me that everything would work out for me—to be brave and positive with my life. He died a few months later.

After his dad's death, the one person who fueled Tony's enthusiasm for life and who encouraged his ambitions to pursue his dreams was his mom, Anna. In talking about Anna, not only with Tony but also with his brother and sister, they were uniform in describing their mother as someone who was totally dedicated to her family. She taught them kindness, perseverance, style, loyalty, and tolerance.

In one discussion I had with Tony's brother, John, who was three years older than Tony, he elaborated on their mother's sense of justice and equality and how she impressed those values on her children.

> "THE AUTHORS AND BOOKS I WAS ENCOURAGED TO READ AS A CHILD INFLUENCED ME GREATLY **IN WALKING TOWARD HUMANITY, RATHER THAN WALKING AWAY FROM IT.**"
>
> —TONY BENNETT

OPPOSITE: *Tony and his older brother, John, Astoria, 1941.* ABOVE: *A Benedetto family photo taken in Pyrites, New York, c. 1930; Tony (first row, far left) sits next to his father; Tony's mother sits behind him.*

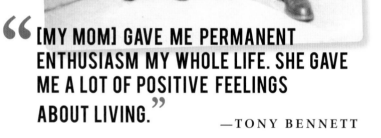

amazing amount of confidence about my personality and my spirit."

One story Tony tells about his childhood captures the closeness and love that was nurtured in the Benedetto Astoria home. As mentioned, Tony was inspired to sing by listening to his father's beautiful voice. Also inspired was Tony's brother, John, who was so talented as a youngster that he became a member of the children's choir organized by the Metropolitan Opera. (Years later, in 2011, in celebration of his eighty-fifth birthday and the release of *Duets II*, and to benefit Exploring the Arts, Tony would perform on the Met's stage. The concert included duets with Aretha Franklin and Elton John, and opened with a video from President Barack Obama.)

"There was a song Bing Crosby sang in the early 1930s called 'My Mom.' My dad sat John and I down and taught us the lyrics, and then he told us he wanted us to serenade our mother after she returned from her long day of work to lift her spirits." In June 1998, Tony Bennett included the song in his concept album *The Playground*, a collection of songs Tony selected to enrich the hearts and minds of children.

In recalling his mother's loyalty to her children, Tony was reminded of an incident that occurred when he was eleven.

After my dad died, my mom was in her early thirties, and our relatives encouraged my mom to start dating. Her family arranged for a gentleman caller to come meet Anna and us children and to have dinner, just to see if there was any chemistry that might lead to a deeper relationship developing. Mom welcomed the man into the living room to meet us and then went to the kitchen to prepare dinner. John and I starting fooling around like typical eleven- and fourteen-year-old boys—we may have been a little loud in our antics. The gentleman, in a raised voice, said, "Hey, why don't you kids tone it down a little? You're being much too loud." My mom came running in from the kitchen and demanded that the man leave—immediately. "No one," she said, "ever speaks to my children in that tone of voice . . . no one!"

"[MY MOM] GAVE ME PERMANENT ENTHUSIASM MY WHOLE LIFE. SHE GAVE ME A LOT OF POSITIVE FEELINGS ABOUT LIVING."

—TONY BENNETT

He said that after he and Tony returned from service in World War II, they stayed up all evening sharing their respective experiences. They both agreed that the deep revulsion they felt for war and the great sense of outrage they shared as they observed racial segregation in the armed forces were the result of the lessons they learned from their father, mother, and family.

When I asked Tony to reflect on his mom's influence on him he said, "I loved her so much! I became the spoiled child because I was the youngest one. So, I couldn't do anything wrong. It used to upset my brother and sister very much. But she just adored me so much, and she gave me an

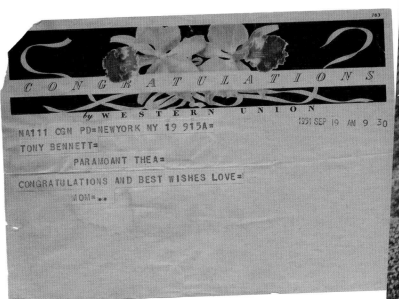

OPPOSITE: *Tony, in uniform, poses with Anna in Astoria, 1946.* ABOVE: *A congratulatory September 19, 1951, telegram from Anna to Tony at the Paramount Theatre, where he was performing in Bob Hope's show.* RIGHT: *Tony and his older sister, Mary, Astoria, 1944.*

Another example of his mom's love and commitment was related to me by Tony's sister, Mary. When Anna was a widow working long, hard hours as a seamstress in the Garment District, the union president called for a rally to encourage the workers to go on strike. Mary said, "My mother was only about five foot five inches and was maybe at tops 105 pounds. She walks up to this big, big man, the union president, and as he looks down on her, she pokes a finger into his chest and yells, 'If we go on strike who's going to feed MY children?'" Mary said the official was left speechless.

Another enduring lesson Tony learned from his mother was to cultivate the highest standards of quality and craftsmanship, no matter what the job at hand entailed. Tony, to this day, recalls how his mother refused to work on inferior garments. His sister described to me how fastidious and particular Anna would be as she prepared meals for her children in the kitchen. She never compromised on the ingredients or the preparation, and as Mary pointed out, "remember, this was during the Depression and mom was a widow." That ethos was ingrained in young Anthony, and it remains at the core of his artistry: never compromise; sing only the best songs surrounded by the finest musicians.

Mary deeply loved her brothers and was often responsible for their care while their mother worked. Because Tony was the youngest sibling, she was especially loving and protective of him, and that relationship also had a profound impact on Tony. I first met Mary in person in 1984, at a Lupus Foundation benefit concert in New York City. I began a soliloquy on the virtues I'd observed over the years in her younger brother, and she gently interrupted me by putting her hand on my arm, saying, "All the wonderful things you're saying about Tony today were apparent to me when he was just a little boy!" Mary not only managed his career at one point but also, through the years, she was a constant presence in Tony's life. She told me how important it was to Tony—when he first began to gain professional success—to realize the dream he had as a young boy and unburden Anna from those twelve-hour workdays. He was finally able to buy her a house and to ensure that, for the rest of her life, she would have the financial security she deserved and the time to spend with her growing family and her friends.

Duke Ellington, God Is Love *watercolor on paper by Tony Bennett. The painting is in the collection of the Smithsonian's National Portrait Gallery.*

"ON A CLEAR DAY YOU CAN SEE FOREVER"

As Tony's fame increased through the 1950s and 1960s, he introduced his family to many iconic entertainers. He would bring people such as Judy Garland, Count Basie, and Duke Ellington to his mother's home for a visit or for one of Anna's delicious homemade dinners. Ellington—who was born in the same year as Anna, 1899, would always take his mom's hand in his and say, "Anna, you get more beautiful looking each time I see you!" It would be one of the highlights of her week. "My mother was so thrilled and charmed by the Duke's grace and elegance," he stated.

Tony had a remarkably close relationship with Ellington, and I once mentioned to Tony that Ellington, in some ways, treated Tony almost as a loving father would treat a son.

"Absolutely!" replied Tony, recounting an oft-told story about Christmas 1965:

I was going through a terrible time in my life because I was going through my divorce. One of the great holidays for me is Christmas. I've always loved Christmas. All of New York City just shines with beautiful lights and a radiant spirit. Everybody's nice and kind to one another and all that—it is just an ideal season. And here I was in a New York City hotel room by myself for the first time in my life, away from my children, my two sons. And I didn't know what to do.

My friend [drummer] Louis Bellson knew how low I was feeling. He was rehearsing with Duke Ellington for the *Concert of Sacred Music* that was to be performed and recorded at the Fifth Avenue Presbyterian Church in New York the day after Christmas. Louis spoke to Ellington about my loneliness and state of mind, and Duke came up with an amazing idea: he would send the choir that was rehearsing with the orchestra for the concert over to my hotel and have them serenade me. I remember it like it was yesterday. I'm in my hotel room and all of a sudden hear some beautiful voices singing. I thought it was the television set, but I knew it wasn't on. I opened up the door and saw that Duke had sent over to the hotel a choir, and they were singing "On a Clear Day You Can See Forever." [Tony recorded this song in August 1970.] And it changed my life. It showed me that there is hope. It had a profound impact on me at that time, and even as I think about over fifty years later, it still inspires me.

I then mentioned to Tony that Ellington also gave him some sage advice about another of Tony's passions, painting.

Well, I was always sketching, and Duke always wanted me to show him what I'd recently drawn. As a young man growing up in DC, his family always encouraged him to paint, and Duke was so talented that he had won a scholarship to attend the Pratt Institute in Brooklyn. He didn't accept it because he wanted to pursue music, but when he saw my sketches and some of my paintings, he was emphatic that I continue to explore art. He told me, "Always do *two* things." Don't do *one*. He said do *two* things. And because I was always itching to paint and learning how to draw and learning how to paint, I took it on. So, now I paint every day, and I study music every day. And I'm doing the two things that I love. It's not work. And I've always been grateful to Duke for his wisdom and encouragement.

On Duke Ellington's 110th birthday, April 29, 2009, the Smithsonian's National Portrait Gallery accepted, as part of its permanent collection, Tony Bennett's portrait of his friend Duke Ellington. There is perhaps no more fitting tribute to Duke's counsel to Tony to commit himself to painting. It's a masterful portrait of the Duke that Tony titled *God Is Love*—appropriately named, as Ellington considered the three Sacred Concerts he wrote at the end of his life to be his "most important work."

* * *

"[TONY BENNETT] IS A BIG BEAUTIFUL MAN. WITH ALL OF HIS GREATNESS, HIS HAT SIZE NEVER NEEDED TO BE LARGER THAN HIS ARTISTIC STATURE. HE'S TOTALLY UNSELFISH, IN A WAY COMPLETELY UNIQUE IN THE THEATER.... WHEN HE BROUGHT BANDS TO WORK WITH HIM, HE BILLED THEIR NAMES, COUNT BASIE AND DUKE ELLINGTON, OVER HIS OWN NAME. THIS IS UNHEARD OF."

—DUKE ELLINGTON, *BILLBOARD* MAGAZINE, "20 YEARS WITH TONY," NOVEMBER 30, 1968

AFTER THE DEEP GRIEF OF LOSING THEIR DAD, Tony and his siblings were engulfed in the arms of the relatives Anna would invite to their Astoria home for Sunday feasts of food and music. Tony has mentioned these weekly rituals as being profound moments in his life, and spoke to me about them as he was celebrating his ninetieth birthday.

After my father died, our relatives were so wonderful. My uncles, aunts, nieces, and nephews—they would come over every Sunday. And after my mom and aunts created a wonderful dinner, the whole group would make a circle around me, my brother, and my sister, and we would entertain my family. . . . After the loss of my dad I remember thinking, *Who am I? What will I do with my life?* I was confused [but] on those Sunday-afternoon gatherings my relatives would get a big kick out of me performing for them, and they'd say, "You know Anthony, you sing very well. And we love the way you paint flowers." . . . Having these relatives tell me who I was (I'm a painter, and I'm a singer! . . . I said "perfect"!) gave me some direction in my life; their kindness and encouragement continues to inspire me at ninety. It's created a passion throughout my life to just improve, improve, practice, practice, practice, and try and get better and better. And it's never stopped. . . . I always tell everyone that I've never worked a day in my life because I'm doing the two things I love. It never feels like work to me, ever.

"MAKE SOMEONE HAPPY"

In December 2005, Kennedy Center Honoree Tony Bennett and the other recipients that year were honored by a pre-ceremony reception hosted at the White House by President George W. Bush and First Lady Laura Bush. In his introductory comments about Tony Bennett, President Bush included Tony's parents and family as being Tony's first inspiration, which eventually led to Tony being named a recipient of one of the country's highest awards for artistic accomplishments:

Tony Bennett once said, "What I try to do is give a performance and have everybody say, 'God, I love that song.'" Well, he's known that satisfaction throughout his career. When you hear the title of a Tony Bennett song, all at once you can hear the man singing it—"Fly Me to the Moon," "The Good Life," "The Best Is Yet to Come," "Just in Time."

This son of New York made his singing debut as a little boy in 1936, standing beside Mayor LaGuardia at the opening of the Triborough Bridge. Much time has passed, and at this point, the Triborough Bridge is showing some age. The little boy who sang that day is still looking pretty good.

Perhaps his biggest professional break came in the late 1940s, when he was opening for Pearl Bailey in Greenwich Village, and she introduced him to Bob Hope. When he learned this young man's name was Anthony Dominick Benedetto, Mr. Hope said, "That's too long for the marquee; let's simplify it and call you Tony Bennett."

Soon he was one of the great nightclub singers, performing through the years with the likes of Duke Ellington and Count Basie and appearing on the *Tonight Show*, as Johnny Carson's first guest. When Tony recorded "I Left My Heart in San Francisco," he won his first GRAMMY, and the song took him from the clubs to Carnegie Hall. From that day to this, he's been playing to sellout crowds. . . .

And it's a symbol of his endurance that this man who was making records when Harry Truman lived in the White House has become a favorite of the MTV generation. As one newspaper declared, "Tony Bennett has not just bridged the generation gap, he demolished it." The vocal style and interpretive skill of Tony Bennett are without equal. And no other singer is held in higher regard by his fellow entertainers. B. B. King once said, "To be near him is a highlight of my life. I've met two presidents in office, I've met the Pope, Pavarotti—and Tony Bennett." Frank Sinatra declared that Tony Bennett was the best singer in his lifetime.

His vocal talent and love for music came from his dad, John Benedetto, who passed away when Tony was ten years old. In his memoir, Tony writes that John was a "very poetic man, full of love and warmth, who sang with a gentle, sensitive voice I can still hear." Tony's mom, Anna, undoubtedly saw those same qualities in her son. He called her "my one guiding star." And in a long life, Anna watched her boy rise to the top and remain there. . . .

Tony Bennett is also a very talented painter, whose work is widely exhibited and admired. He's a deeply committed humanitarian. He's a man of character who

served in the US Army in World War II, and he marched for civil rights with Martin Luther King Jr.

Of his career, Tony Bennett has said, "The audience has been beautiful to me." And the sentiment is entirely mutual. Everybody likes the man. He's been aptly described as "the kind of celebrity who cabdrivers call by his first name." We're joyful that he remains a friendly presence in American life, an entertainer still at the top of his game, and a voice we love to hear.

Kennedy Center honoree Tony Bennett on the red carpet before the gala in Washington, DC, December 27, 2005.

That sense of joy—expressed through, as President Bush mentioned, "a voice we love to hear"—has shone through each time Tony Bennett has been in a recording studio. This joyfulness and depth of feeling inhabit so many of Tony's recordings, and they are the essential elements that I—and millions of others—find so attractive and compelling in his music. After naming Tony the "best singer in the business" in the April 1965 *Life* magazine cover story, Frank Sinatra went on to give a couple of reasons for his assessment: "For my money, Tony Bennett is the best exponent of a song. He excites me when I watch him. He moves me. He's the singer who gets across what the composer has in mind, and probably a little more." This observation, coming from one of Tony's boyhood idols and adulthood friends, captures the ingredients in the Bennett recording catalogue that separate his artistry from so many others—that "little bit more" that Sinatra heard in Tony's singing is the essence of who Bennett is as a singer: an "honest" storyteller.

* * *

THROUGH THE YEARS OF PLAYING PERHAPS thousands of Bennett recordings, I've had many radio listeners ask me, "Does Tony Bennett write the songs he sings?" That "spark" you discern when he's singing "Keep Smiling at Trouble" or that empathy you feel when listening to him sing Charlie Chaplin's song "Smile"—it just seems to the listener that the singer and the song are one.

Someone who expressed Tony's ability to get across what the composer has in mind is playwright/screenwriter Tony Kushner, a Pulitzer Prize winner. In May 2010, both he and Tony Bennett were awarded honorary degrees from New York City's renowned Juilliard School of Music. Fifty years earlier, in the summer of 1960, composer Cy Coleman and lyricist Carolyn Leigh, two of Tony's favorite composers, had brought to his attention a song they'd just written called "The Best Is Yet to Come." They didn't have to convince Tony to record the song—he loved it. The opti-

mism and the excitement about the "possibilities" in the future matched the Tony Bennett spirit. It continues to be one of his signature songs, and it always receives a strong response from worldwide audiences. Kushner, during his Juilliard speech, identified the impact of the singer and song becoming one:

I'm terrifically honored to be here, I'm grateful to have been asked to speak to you, and I don't want to begin by giving offense, but I think you guys are crazy. Why on earth did you ask me to give this speech when instead you could've asked Tony Bennett to sing "The Best Is Yet to Come"? My speech is going to be 10 to 12 minutes. "The Best Is Yet to Come," as Mr. Bennett sings it, is 2 minutes and 35 seconds. . . . So not only would you be out of here and on to whatever awaits you at least 7 minutes and 25 seconds sooner, but you'd *know*, if you'd asked Tony Bennett to sing that song for you, beyond all argument or doubt you'd *know* that whatever it is that awaits you, it's a real good bet the best is yet to come. What more could anyone ask from a commencement speech? I can't imagine there's ever been a commencement speaker who shouldn't have been replaced by Tony Bennett singing that song—well, maybe not Ralph Waldo Emerson, but pretty much everyone else. . . . He'd have told you, beyond all argument or doubt: "You *think* you've seen the sun, but you ain't seen it shine!"

"IF I RULED THE WORLD"

The "soul" that informs Tony Bennett's singing has successfully connected his voice to millions of fans for over seven decades. But it is not just contained to his life as an entertainer, it is also manifested in his personal life by, among other things, his response to racism, poverty, and injustice. After losing his beloved dad, one of the most profound discoveries Tony learned early on is that life is a gift, something to be cherished and defended. "I grew up in a home where we were taught by example to never judge someone by the color of their skin, their religion, or how much money they had," he told me when we talked about the shock he first experienced when he served in a segregated World War II US Army. "My grandfather wanted the family to settle in Astoria after emigrating from Italy, because of its diversity. I was aware, to a degree, of racial prejudice, but in Astoria there were people representing so many nationalities. My grandfather said, 'In Italy I grew up with just Italians; America is different—you can live with people from all kinds of backgrounds.'"

Along with the many celebrations and tributes to Tony Bennett as he commemorated his ninetieth birthday, Tony's life as a civil rights advocate was acknowledged by one of his closest friends, Harry Belafonte. Early in his life, this son of Caribbean immigrants, who became an internationally recognized entertainer and civil rights activist, was inspired by the life and artistry of singer Paul Robeson and the writing of W. E. B. Du Bois. A defining moment in Harry's life occurred in the late 1950s, when he and Dr. Martin Luther King Jr. became friends. In addition to his financial support for various civil rights groups, Belafonte helped to organize rallies and protests that resulted in raising the country's consciousness to the sin of racial discrimination and inequality. In 2016, he reflected on Tony Bennett's early support of the civil rights struggle (see page 43).

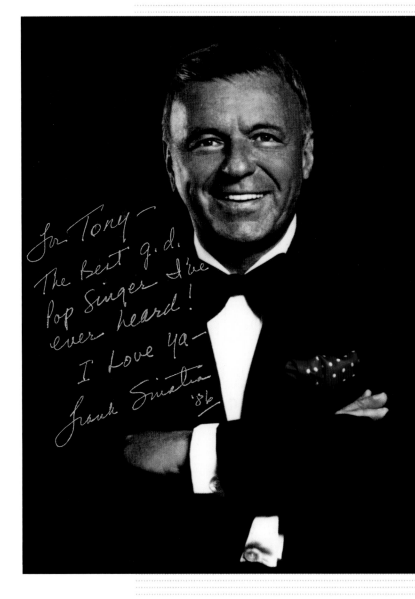

OPPOSITE: *Tony Bennett receives an honorary degree at the Juilliard School of Music's commencement ceremony at Alice Tully Hall, Lincoln Center, New York, May 21, 2010.* ABOVE: *A photograph of Frank Sinatra, which he autographed in 1986: "For Tony—The best g.d. pop singer I've ever heard! I love ya."*

Speaking truth to power is not always an easy task, especially among those who have achieved celebrity. Often many of us who are called on to use our public approval to support causes that are not always without conflict must measure the cost of such a commitment carefully. There are but a handful of courageous individuals who are not intimidated by the negative consequence. Their moral clarity and deep caring for fellow beings unable to stave off the cruelty of those who hold them in conditions of human suffering gives them the courage to speak out and to stand up. Tony is one of these few. I know this side of Tony's caring because I have on occasion called upon his goodwill.

In 1965, America was in the midst of great political turmoil. Just a few short months after the historic demonstration in Washington, DC, which gave Dr. King the platform for his remarkable "I Have a Dream" speech, the March on Washington was responded to by violent racist forces in the state of Alabama, who bombed a black church in Birmingham, Alabama, taking the lives of four little black Sunday school girls. The citizens in Selma, along with Dr. Martin Luther King, decided that they would march to the state capital of Montgomery to protest the persistent violence against black citizens. Dr. King called upon the citizens of America to participate in and be supportive of this campaign.

I was charged with the responsibility of insuring there would be a strong presence of highly popular artists in support of this demonstration. It was Tony Bennett who was the first to respond to my call. Tony understood that by making this commitment, there was a possibility of potential fallout and that many disgruntled Americans might boycott his work, causing serious ramifications to his career. Because of his moral commitment to justice and his deep belief that segregation was unacceptable, Tony not only agreed to appear at a great concert at the Selma rally but used his influence to attract the participation of other artists of the period. Dr. King was most aware of how artists were put upon because of their support to our cause and often expressed his indebtedness to their courage. He said because of their commitment, the success of our cause was assured.

Tony was always one of the first to answer the call.

On the occasion of this writing, Tony is celebrating his ninetieth year. He is just a few weeks older than I, a fact he used to constantly remind me of with glee, but now that we are in the winter of our years, he hardly speaks of it. Tony has endured far better than many of us. His popularity is undiminished. His art is a source of constant joy. I have long since stepped away from the performing arts, and rarely does that fact occupy my thoughts until I see Tony in his space. What a joy!

OPPOSITE: *Tony Bennett and Harry Belafonte pose for a portrait during the 2013 Amy Winehouse Foundation Inspiration Awards and Gala at the Waldorf Astoria in New York, March 21, 2013.*

On August 28, 2017, Tony and Susan were invited by Lady Gaga to attend her New York concert at Citi Field in Queens, part of her *Joanne* World Tour. When she acknowledged Tony's presence in the stadium, she reminded her young audience that Tony had marched with Dr. King and that he had, throughout his life, quietly done much work for civil rights and other causes that defended justice. "Tony always talks to me about how it's important to stand up for what you believed in and to help other people."

I spoke with Tony in February 2007, the week he was an inductee (along with Sidney Poitier and the late boxer Joe Louis) in the Civil Rights Walk of Fame, which is located in downtown Atlanta in the plaza of the Martin Luther King Jr. National Historic Site. The walk was established in 2004, and it contains the footprints, preserved in granite, of the people who the organizers call the "foot soldiers" of the civil rights movement in America. Tony was thrilled with the honor and said it was actually a walk he had as a child that helped inform his views on race in America.

When I was very young, I had relatives in Manhattan, and I used to visit with them and listen to Bing Crosby records. After visiting them one Sunday afternoon, I left their home and decided that I would walk back to Astoria from Manhattan, and on the way, of all things, I got lost. I just kept walking and walking, and suddenly found myself in Harlem. At that time, I was being told by some people that as a white boy, I shouldn't be in that neighborhood; it was dangerous. And what a revelation it was to me that night. Here I was, this little lost kid, and I found Harlem to be safest place I've ever been to. Everybody was very kind to me; I was not frightened about being in Harlem but scared that it was getting late and I didn't know how to get back to my home. There wasn't one person who didn't try to help me find my way back to Queens. They eliminated all the fear I had inside me at the time. And it taught me many years later the folly of racial prejudice.

We have a very unusual country; a great, great country, because it's one of a kind. . . . Its people come from every race, every nationality, every religion. I had learned in my home that here in the United States, we should strive to eliminate all bigotry because we're all allowed to live here with the promise of freedom and equality. And we could teach the rest of the world by our actions, by setting an example that we get along. And that's what THEY should do. That's what Dr. King and all of those marchers were trying to teach us through their activities.

The day Tony's footprints were added to the Civil Rights Walk of Fame, the walk's creator, Xernona Clayton, told the audience, "The rains will come and wash away the debris . . . but your footsteps and contributions will stand forever."

As the Selma to Montgomery march concluded on March 25, 1965 (several weeks after America's participation in the Vietnam War escalated as US troops came ashore in Da Nang), America was embracing a "musical expression" of Tony Bennett's sense of humanity—a song heard on the radio that spoke to the country's widespread discontent. The March 27 *Billboard*'s Top 40 chart contained records by, among others, the Beatles, the Temptations, the Supremes, Roy Orbison, the Dave Clark Five, the Four Tops, the Moody Blues . . . and Tony Bennett's recording of "If I Ruled the World." When I played it on the radio, I always thought of it as a "protest" song. Listening to this record in the context of the stress and anxiety beginning to engulf the country at that time, Tony's voice seemed to break through the domestic tumult to give voice to an ideal world and offer hope.

The Tony Bennett catalogue is a rich repository of songs and iconic performances. I'm not aware of any great American standard/jazz singer who, through his music, has communicated such a positive and enduring view of life. Many of the song titles in the catalogue reflect the heart, soul, and spirit of his oeuvre; just a short list includes "Life Is Beautiful," "The Best Thing to Be Is a Person," "Keep Smiling at Trouble," "Smile," "Make Someone Happy," "A Child Is Born," "Home Is the Place," "Live for Life," "You Must Believe in Spring," "What a Wonderful World," "Love Is the Thing," "Days of Love," "The Best Is Yet to Come," "For Once in My Life," "The Good Things in Life," and "I'll Begin Again." When composer Alec Wilder heard the Tony Bennett/Bill Evans recording of "A Child Is Born," he observed, "Tony performs 'A Child Is Born' with special tenderness. He gives to each word a verbal image, extremely sensitive respect and lovingness."

Dizzy Gillespie once said, "I think Tony's spirituality is so profound in his performance that it cuts through everything superfluous, and what's left is raw soulfulness. Because his philosophy in life is so basic, the moment he opens his mouth to sing you know exactly what he is—a prince."

Among the recent GRAMMY Award–winning tribute projects Tony has recorded is his 2002 *What a Wonderful World* collaboration with k.d. lang to honor one of his idols, Louis Armstrong. When asked during an ABC-TV *Primetime* interview in 2002 about what she learned from the experience of recording with Tony she said, "I was amazed by his phrasing as he sings. But perhaps the most import-

ant thing I've learned from Tony Bennett is to *love* life. He loves life, and he's taught me to love life."

The spirit of the song "What a Wonderful World" and Tony Bennett's view of life are very compatible. Louis Armstrong, born under very difficult circumstances in 1901 in New Orleans and subjected to racial prejudice at home, became one of America's most important cultural ambassadors. He never gave up the belief that given the chance most people will do the right thing. He, and Tony, espoused the belief that music is a gift that brings people to a conscious place that directs their actions and helps create that "Wonderful World."

In 2000, the United Nations honored Tony as a recipient of their Citizen of the World award, and in 2007 he received a United Nations Humanitarian Award. On that occasion, on the evening of June 19, he performed for many top UN officials at a concert held in the Swiss Embassy in Georgetown. The following morning, the UN High Commissioner for Refugees presented Tony with the award for his long-standing support of UN activities, including fronting a fundraising concert to support the many innocent victims of violence in Darfur, Sudan.

Tony Bennett sings as other inductees listen, during an induction ceremony held by the International Civil Rights Walk of Fame in Atlanta, February 26, 2007.

3
" *the* ART SPIRIT "

Tony Bennett called me one afternoon in the late summer of September 2016. He had just returned to his apartment after spending the day painting in his art studio, both of which overlook Central Park in New York City. We were talking about Ella Fitzgerald when he suddenly exclaimed, "Excuse me Dick, but I have to interrupt to tell you what I'm looking at as I gaze out the window and over at the park. The leaves have just started turning from green to gold; the sun is creating beautiful light shafts that are surrounding the skyscrapers, I can see this all the way up to Harlem, and the sky is a beautiful dark blue." He said this with such joy and such excitement that I commented, "Tony this is the ninetieth time you've witnessed summer turning into fall and from the enthusiasm and sense of discovery I hear in your voice, it sounds as though this is the very first time you've seen this natural beauty!"

Tony's lifelong relationship with Central Park—which began when he was a student at the High School of Industrial Arts—has been a constant source of inspiration to his painting and music. He told me,

> The park really connected me with a love of the natural world. The trees, flowers, the openness of the area were so attractive to me. My high school was located on Seventy-Ninth Street, right down the block from the Metropolitan Museum of Art, and we were allowed to go there [during school hours if schoolwork was completed], and I would often visit after school, too. And, as important to me, we were also allowed to go to Central Park. And to this day, I still paint in Central Park all the time. Susan and I, along with our little doggie Happy, visit the park often. I love it. . . . Everybody thinks of New York City as just one big skyscraper after another. And they're right, except Central Park, which is all nature. And I never can get over how beautiful it is. You can see the changes in the four seasons through the nature. It not only inspires my painting and music but it inspires my life.

PREVIOUS PAGES: *Tony Bennett performs at the Latin Casino, Philadelphia, 1963.* ABOVE: *As a teenager, Tony attended the High School of Industrial Arts, down the street from the Metropolitan Museum of Art; here he is at age fifteen with his brother, John, in Astoria, 1941.* OPPOSITE: *Tony in his studio overlooking Central Park, 1995.*

"NATURE IS THE BOSS!"

—TONY BENNETT

When Tony was a youngster, his dad would take him for long walks through their Astoria neighborhood when that area, in the early 1930s, was still fairly rural (by New York standards). John Benedetto would have Tony gaze up at the nighttime sky, and he would explain to young Anthony where our planet was located in the vast cosmos. To this day Tony recalls the summer night he and his father were out walking and witnessed a display of the aurora borealis, or Northern Lights.

"You have to remember that at the time Astoria was not as built up as it is today," Tony noted. "What I saw in the sky that evening was extraordinary and indelible in my mind!"

John Benedetto explained to his nine-year-old son that what they were seeing was a cosmic experience and that all of life on this planet is somehow connected to the "great cosmos." What dazzled young Anthony were the colors: pink and pale green, blue and violet. Not too long after this experience, Tony recounted that "I had this very vivid dream where my dad and I were holding hands and walking together through what appeared to be a valley. It was a dream that seemed so real—not only for the colors that surrounded us but I also clearly remember the peace and tranquility I felt, secure in my father's love and surrounded by nature." The tranquility, the beauty, and most especially the colors he experienced in this dream have stayed with him all of his life, and—he believes, as he paints in his studio above Central Park—has helped inspire his love of painting.

"THE COLORS OF MY LIFE"

While studying painting as an adult, Tony was introduced to a book titled *The Art Spirit* by Robert Henri. This volume, which focuses on the essential elements of creating, deepened his curiosity about and appreciation of the natural world and continues to influence his approach to his "creative life" both in the art studio and in the recording studio.

Portrait of Robert Henri, c. 1900; Henri's classic 1923 book The Art Spirit *has been an inspiration to Tony throughout his life.*

Henri was a leading member of the early twentieth-century art movement known as the Ashcan School, and an influential teacher at the Art Students League of New York. The artist, who died at the age of sixty-four in 1929, was a charismatic man who had a highly developed ability to articulate aspects of painting beyond mechanics and technique; he had refined and poetic insights into the meaning of creativity and the human impulse to communicate, through art, the deepest expressions of man's place on earth. *The Art Spirit*, first published in 1923, is a collection of some of Henri's lectures in addition to excerpts from his personal letters. Some consider this work to be as insightful and influential as Leonardo da Vinci's notebooks.

"DO WHATEVER YOU DO INTENSELY. THE ARTIST IS THE MAN WHO LEAVES THE CROWD AND GOES PIONEERING. WITH HIM THERE IS AN IDEA WHICH IS HIS LIFE."

—ROBERT HENRI, *THE ART SPIRIT*, 1923

Henri, during one of his lectures, said: "Sometimes within reading the first two pages of a book you know you've found a brother." In *The Art Spirit*, Tony found a brother. Several years ago he gave me a copy of this classic volume. After the publication in 2012 of Tony's book *Life Is a Gift*, I mentioned to him how much I enjoyed the lovely dedication page: "I would like to dedicate this book to my wonderful family, my lovely wife, Susan Benedetto, and to Robert Henri's *The Art Spirit*." Tony replied,

In my lifetime, it's the best book ever written to capture the true "art spirit." One of the profound lessons I've learned from reading it is that anyone who does anything well . . . anyone who's dedicated and invests their love and gifts to the task at hand . . . is an artist. It's not that they paint or that they sing or they dance or that perhaps their work is part of the Smithsonian. That has nothing to do with it. It's anybody who does anything very well and dedicates their life with full integrity about going toward quality. In other words we *all* have the capacity to do great things.

As in Tony's musical life—where he sought inspiration by associating with artists such as Bill Evans, Duke Ellington, and Count Basie—Tony's life as a painter has been enriched by interacting with other painters he's met and painted with at institutions like the Art Students League of New York. He's studied with watercolorist Charles Reid and others, but perhaps his most enduring relationship with a painter has been the wonderful and mutually inspiring friendship he has developed with renowned artist Everett Raymond Kinstler, who has painted more than twelve hundred portraits, including the official portraits of presidents Ford and Reagan. In one interview I did with Tony in 2006, he talked about how serendipitous their meeting had been:

After finishing at the High School of Industrial Arts, serving in World War II, and then launching a career as a singer . . . many years later, I met an agent in the music business. He said, "You know, I have a relative who's a great painter. . . . He's the most famous portrait painter in America, Everett Raymond Kinstler. Would you like to meet him?" And I said, "Sure I would." So, he introduced me and took me to Everett's studio in New York, and when I walked in, he said, "You're Benedetto, and your birthday is August 3." And he told me how old I was at the time. This was like at least forty years ago, and of all things, he went to the same school I did. He wasn't in the same class I was in, but he heard that I was starting to get popular. And other former schoolmates told him, "You know, Tony Bennett is really Anthony Benedetto who used to go to this school." He knew who I was and became my teacher in painting for the last forty-five years now. He's a great, great friend and a beautiful artist.

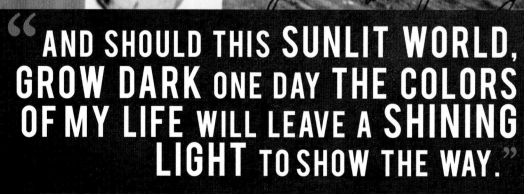

"AND SHOULD THIS **SUNLIT WORLD**, **GROW DARK** ONE DAY **THE COLORS** OF MY LIFE WILL LEAVE A **SHINING LIGHT** TO SHOW THE WAY."

—"THE COLORS OF MY LIFE," LYRICS BY MICHAEL STEWART, COMPOSED BY CY COLEMAN, ORIGINALLY WRITTEN FOR THE 1980 BROADWAY MUSICAL *BARNUM*

About seventy years ago, Anthony Benedetto and I were fellow students at the High School of Industrial Arts, in New York City. This attests to the fact he was deeply interested in becoming an artist at an early age.

He also was possessed of a remarkable talent as a singer and, as Tony Bennett, became an iconic figure in American popular music for seven decades.

During his adult and professional years he has led a double life: as singer-interpreter extraordinaire and gifted painter and artist.

In the past forty years, I have observed and admired him painting almost on a daily basis. His paints, notably watercolors, are a constant companion when he travels. His career has taken him around the world, and his paintings have reflected his moods, impressions, and reactions to the visual and colorful images he sees. Painting the streets of San Francisco, London, and New York, the skies and imagery of Europe, the shades and atmosphere of Asia, and the peoples from countries around the world, he is continuously stimulated, and he paints to record his impressions. His studio view of Central Park, New York City, in all seasons, remains a personal source of inspiration. And his sketchbook is filled with drawings of his fellow musicians, friends, and people he draws and records in the daily life around him.

Talking with our mutual friend, Dave Brubeck, about Tony's paintings, I mentioned how much Tony has affected my own work through his music, the importance of expressing the meaning of the words to convey the feelings, and how colors are related to the keyboard and notes. Dave smiled and said, "That's how I approach my piano."

His art, so much a part of his life, always displays an innocence and sense of the narrative. He is constantly reading, studying, taking art classes, going to galleries and museums, trying to improve his craft.

For my part, I know I am a better artist for his insights, interest, and valued friendship. He has taught and continues to teach me through example.

One of my favorite Tony Bennett songs, composed by his friend Cy Coleman, is "The Colors of My Life." The lyrics [by Michael Stewart] might well have been written for Tony.

Tony poses for a portrait by his friend and mentor Everett Raymond Kinstler, in Kinstler's New York Studio, 1995.

"THE URGE TO EXPRESS MYSELF GOES INTO MY PAINTINGS AND MY SINGING. I SEARCH FOR SONGS THAT WILL EXPLAIN WHAT I'VE LEARNED ABOUT LIFE AND WHAT I FEEL ABOUT LIFE. AND THE PAINTINGS AND DRAWINGS ARE KIND OF A VISUAL DIARY."

—TONY BENNETT

Tony's artistry often simultaneously and effortlessly inhabits both the art studio and the recording studio; there are many instances in his oeuvre of one of his gifts influencing the other. To my ears I can't think of a recording artist who has more consistently sung with such deep insight into the natural world than Tony Bennett. The years he has spent studying flowers, trees, the ocean, and the sky, and trying to commit to canvas what his eyes and heart have seen—chronicling the passing seasons—give many of his recordings a special radiance. A short list of expressions from "a man for all seasons" would include "A Time for Love," "Autumn Leaves," "Snowfall," and "Spring in Manhattan." Over the years Tony recorded countless other nature-inspired recordings, from "Walkabout," "Soon It's Gonna Rain," "Isn't This a Lovely Day?," "When the Sun Comes Out," "Over the Sun," "Over the Rainbow," and "I'll Bring You a Rainbow," to "It Was Written in the Stars," "So Many Stars," "Quiet Nights of Quiet Stars," "The Shining Sea," "Once in a Garden," "It's So Peaceful in the Country," "A Sleepin' Bee," and "House of Flowers." In each of these

OPPOSITE: *Tony surrounded by his paintings and drawings at a New York City studio, 2004.*

RIGHT: *Tony Bennett in the studio recording "Yesterday I Heard the Rain," 1968.*

performances you can see *and* feel what Tony Bennett is singing about.

Tony once told me about an afternoon spent with composer João Gilberto and Gilberto's nine-year-old son. Gilberto—along with Luiz Bonfá, Antônio Carlos Jobim, and Astrud Gilberto (who sang "The Girl from Ipanema")—all became fast friends with Tony when they met him on his first trip to perform in Brazil in 1961. Tony fell in love with Brazilian music, and in December 1962 he recorded some of the first vocal bossa nova music in North America when he sang Jobim's song, "Quiet Nights of Quiet Stars" (called "Corcovado" in Brazil). The song, with lyrics by Gene Lees, was released in 1963 on Tony's album *I Wanna Be Around*. A few years later, when João was in New York, Tony invited him and his son to visit Tony's home recording studio. It was such a memorable afternoon with João and Tony playing for the sheer joy of it. "All of a sudden I looked over and noticed that the young boy had tears rolling down his cheeks. I was so concerned—I stopped singing and said, 'João, is everything alright with your son? Why is he crying?' Gilberto spoke to the child for a moment in Portuguese and then turned to me with a big smile on his face and he said, 'My son has tears of joy! The music we're creating is making him so happy he can only cry!'"

* * *

AMONG THE MOST REWARDING musical collaborations over Tony's seven decades in the recording studio were the times he was able to work with composer/conductor Robert Farnon. An example of the artist and singer becoming one is Bennett's recording of "Country Girl." The song, written in 1966 by Farnon, is based on the haunting and vivid 1805 poem "The Solitary Reaper" by English Romantic poet William Wordsworth. Tony recorded "Country Girl" in November 1966, with an arrangement by Marion Evans, and it was released in 1967 on the album *Tony Makes It*

Happen. Tony's performance indelibly captured the poetry contained in this song. Years later, his moving rendition of "Country Girl" was included in a memorial service for Farnon held in 2005 at St. Paul's Church in London.

The cover of Tony Makes It Happen, *1967; the album includes the moving Robert Farnon song "Country Girl."*

"CLIMB EV'RY MOUNTAIN"

In Tony's art studio hangs one of his favorite Duke Ellington quotes: "Rule #1 NEVER GIVE UP; Rule #2, see #1." With that spirited approach to living, Tony has achieved one of the seemingly most elusive accomplishments in life: he enjoys great physical and emotional health at ninety-one (he goes to the gym several times a week!), and he is serene, content, and still relevant—continuing to open ears and hearts to the songbooks of great American standards and jazz. When asked how his lasting success was possible, he spreads the credit around: "Well, I've had great training. I had a wonderful supporting family as a child. I had good teachers at the American Theatre Wing when I came out of the service

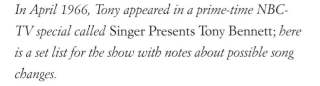

THE TONY BENNETT SHOW
RUNDOWN

4/28/66

	INDIVIDUAL TIMINGS	ACCUMULATIVE TIMINGS
1. OVERTURE	1:45	
2. "WHO CAN I TURN TO"		
3. TITLE AND BILLBOARDS		
4. COMMERCIAL NO. 1		
5. "I CAN'T GIVE YOU ANYTHING BUT LOVE" *WHEN YOURE SMILING*	2:20	
6. "THE SHADOW OF YOUR SMILE" (with Paul Horne) *BECAUSE OF YOU*		
7. "ONE FOR MY BABY" "IT HAD TO BE YOU" (with Bobby Hackett) "ONE FOR MY BABY" - (Reprise)		
8. "IF I RULED THE WORLD" *SHADOW OF YOUR SMILE*		
9. "SING YOU SINNERS"		
10. "BECAUSE OF YOU" *IF I RULED THE WORLD*		
11. "FASCINATING RHYTHM" (with Buddy Rich)		
12. COMMERCIAL NO. 2		
13. SAN FRANCISCO SEGMENT "SAN FRANCISCO" "JUST IN TIME" "TASTE OF HONEY" "ONCE UPON A TIME" "SAN FRANCISCO" (Reprise)		

In April 1966, Tony appeared in a prime-time NBC-TV special called Singer Presents Tony Bennett; *here is a set list for the show with notes about possible song changes.*

after the Second World War. They told me how to survive and taught me how to take care of myself and to be myself, and try not to imitate any other singers . . . and I've maintained that throughout the years."

Tony learned another enduring life lesson in 1966, which he has communicated several times over the years. He'd been asked by the Singer Company, maker of sewing machines, to star in a major prime-time television special they were sponsoring on NBC.

> **" I JUST LOVE THE FACT THAT, IN AN ERA WHERE EVERYTHING'S BASED ON YOUTH, I CAN COMMUNICATE WITH EVERYBODY: THE YOUNG, THE MIDDLE-AGED, AND THE OLD, LIKE ME. AND ALSO TODAY I'M SO INSPIRED BY MY FAMILY'— MY WIFE, SUSAN, MY SONS AND DAUGHTERS, AND MY BEAUTIFUL GRANDCHILDREN. I'M VERY CONTENT."**
>
> —TONY BENNETT

I agreed to the idea but only if they allowed me to have total artistic control. The president of the company and the gentleman who would be the executive producer, Alfred diScipio, was such an enlightened person. He asked me who I wanted to have on the show, and I said how about Ralph Burns to conduct the orchestra and duets with me and Bobby Hackett, the Paul Horn Quintet, Milt Jackson, Cándido Camero, and Buddy Rich. Al responded, "Done!"

During one of the rehearsal breaks, Buddy Rich and I were engaged in a very deep discussion about music and life. I told him that I always dwelled on the mistakes I'd made in my life—professionally and personally. He straightened me right out: "Tony, there is an old expression in show business that is incorrect. Everyone always says 'you're only as good as your last show.' That is totally wrong! You're only as good as your *next* show. . . . You should have learned from any mistakes in your last show and not repeat them in your next show. If you apply this to your personal and professional life, you'll never stop learning and you'll always be on a journey to be the best Tony Bennett you can be!" To this day his wisdom is something I try to live by.

On August 4, 2017, Tony performed a concert at Chicago's famed Ravinia outdoor music festival, the first full day of his ninety-first year. The award-winning *Chicago Tribune* arts critic Howard Reich filed a report the following day entitled "Yes, Tony Bennett Still Sings Grandly at 91," noting that "Even if Tony Bennett hadn't turned ninety-one the day before . . . his concert Friday night would have been one for the record books. Not simply because he sang more than two dozen songs at something close to perfection, but also because of the expressive breadth of his work, the insights of his lyric reading, the impeccable quality of his pitch, and his singular way of shaping a melody."

To have received a review like Mr. Reich's at thirty-five years old would almost certainly mean your place in music was secure, but no one in popular music to this point in our cultural history has received such praise at ninety-one. Later in 2017, on November 15, Tony would be the recipient of the annual Library of Congress Gershwin Prize for Popular Song—the first interpretive singer to be acknowledged with this coveted distinction. How appropriate! In April 1949, Tony Bennett—at that time still known as "Joe Bari"—made his first recording: the 1924 Gershwin classic "Fascinating Rhythm."

During the course of his unprecedented career as a recording artist, Tony Bennett has committed his studio efforts to singing wonderful melodies with meaningful stories—music created by craftspeople who had something of significance to convey in their songs. As Robert Henri so eloquently wrote in *The Art Spirit*, "If you want to know how to do a thing you must first have a complete desire to do that thing. Then go to kindred spirits . . . learn from their successes and failures and add your quota. . . . With this technical knowledge you may go forward, expressing through the play of forms the music that is in you."

OPPOSITE: *Tony celebrated his ninety-first birthday with a concert at the famed Ravinia music festival in Chicago; here, his acclaimed 1996 painting of the festival,* Ravinia Stars.

Librarian of Congress Dr. Carla Hayden presents Tony Bennett with the 2017 Gershwin Prize for Popular Song during the Gershwin concert at DAR Constitution Hall, Washington, DC, November 15, 2017.

" I LIKE THE SEARCH OF GETTING INTO THE SUBCONSCIOUS, OF IMMERSING MYSELF INTO THE CREATIVE PROCESS. I'M SO LUCKY TO BE ABLE TO DO TWO THINGS, PAINTING AND SINGING, WHICH KEEPS THE CREATIVE PROCESS ROLLING ALL THE TIME. "

—TONY BENNETT

4

IN *the* RECORDING STUDIO I: 1950–1960s

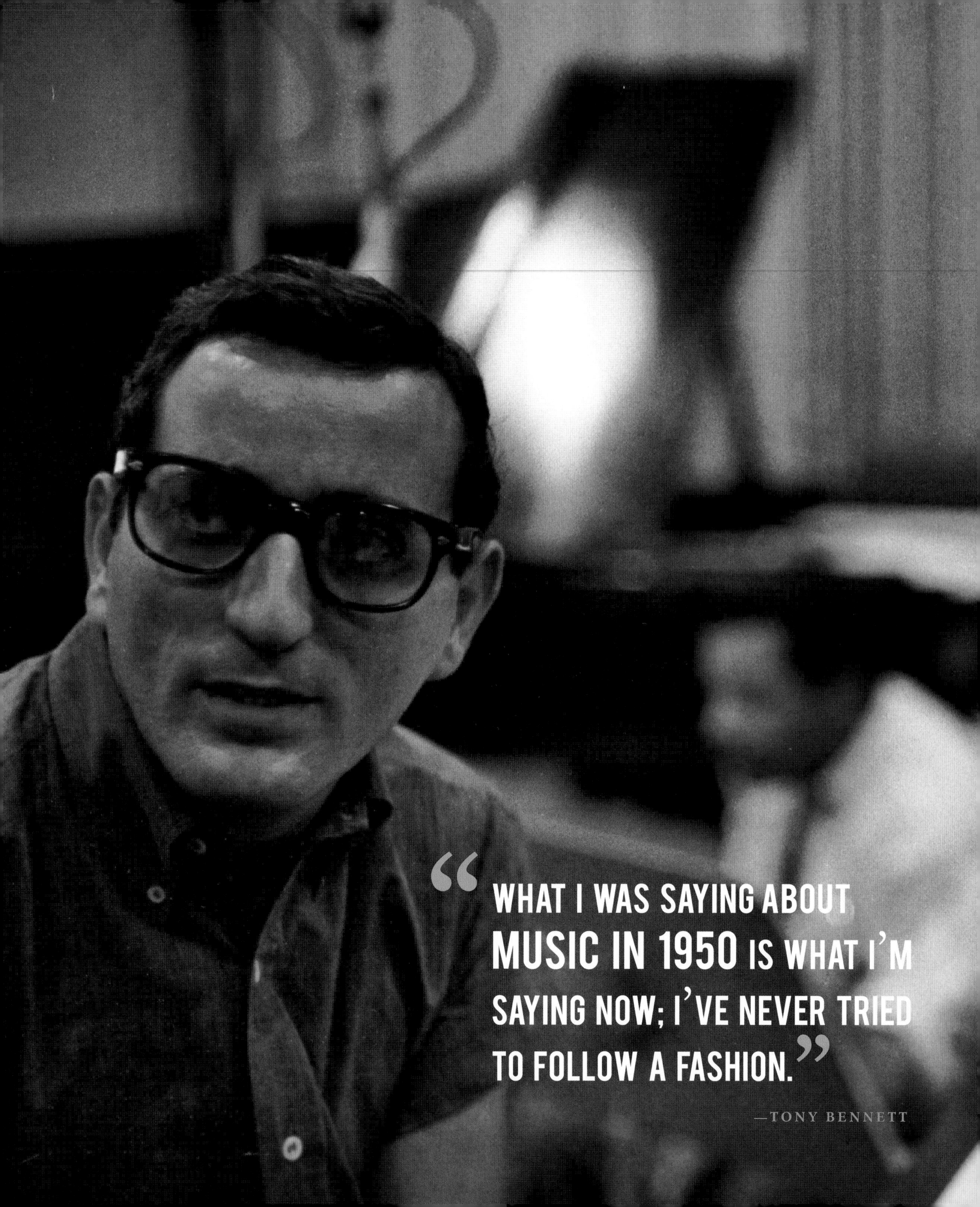

> **WHAT I WAS SAYING ABOUT MUSIC IN 1950 IS WHAT I'M SAYING NOW; I'VE NEVER TRIED TO FOLLOW A FASHION.**
>
> —TONY BENNETT

In November 2017, Tony Bennett became the first interpretive singer to be awarded the highly coveted Library of Congress Gershwin Prize (see page 59) He'd been named a living legend by the nation's library in 2000, but the Gershwin Prize, established to honor the legacy and genius of one of America's popular song composers, George Gershwin, was especially significant because not only has Tony performed so many definitive versions of the classic songs that constitute "The Great American Songbook," but no performer has been more consistent in articulating the importance of this body of work.

"I had a great advantage I believe," he told me recently, "in having grown up when so many of America's greatest popular composers were at the peak of their creativity. They wrote songs that have endured through so much change in our culture. Their songs are not old—they're great."

He added, "There was a musical renaissance period in the 1920s, '30s, and '40s—the first "talkie" film was a musical, *The Jazz Singer,* in 1927; songs were being written for Broadway shows; and radio carried these songs into the ears of Americans of all ages. Beautiful melodies and intelligent lyrics written by George and Ira Gershwin, Irving Berlin, Cole Porter, Harold Arlen, Hoagy Carmichael, and Jerome Kern."

Tony Bennett has been perhaps the most passionate voice in reminding us of the noble way this musical legacy represents America. "I play in China. I play in Norway, Sweden, Spain, Germany, and Italy, in North and South America, and everywhere I perform these citizens of the world cheer our American standards!"

The 2017 Gershwin Prize celebration on November 15 at DAR Constitution Hall demonstrated the unifying power of Tony's artistry and the music he represents. In one of the most divisive periods in our recent history, members of both parties of Congress stood and cheered as a galaxy of performers—Chris Botti, Michael Bublé, Gloria Estefan, Wé McDonald, Michael Feinstein, Savion Glover, Josh Groban, Brian Stokes Mitchell, Lukas Nelson, Vanessa Williams, Wynton Marsalis, Stevie Wonder—honored Tony in both word and song.

PREVIOUS PAGES: *Tony Bennett and Mitch Miller (next to Tony) at the CBS 30th Street Studio, New York, September 19, 1957.* OPPOSITE: *Tony in the CBS 30th Street Studio, New York, recording the* Beat of My Heart *album, October 1957.* RIGHT: *A standing ovation for Tony as he receives the 2017 Gershwin Prize for Popular Song at DAR Constitution Hall, Washington, DC, November 15, 2017.*

After Democratic and Republican leaders joined Librarian Carla Hayden on stage to present the prize to Tony, Dr. Hayden told the audience, "[Tony Bennett] has given us music that lasts and continues to be relevant and meaningful, generation after generation—music that thrills our hearts each time we hear it." The members of Congress returned to their seats, and Tony capped the evening by singing three Gershwin classics. As he began the verse to "Our Love Is Here to Stay," the audience erupted in laughter. It sounded like Tony Bennett was speaking directly to them through the wit and wisdom of the Gershwin brothers almost eighty years ago:

> The more I read the papers
> The less I comprehend
> The world and all its capers
> and how it all will end.
> Nothing seems to be lasting, but that
>   isn't our affair.
> We've got something permanent,
> I mean in the way we care.
> It's very clear
> our love is here to stay.

Fred Astaire, another master interpreter of America's classic popular songs, has long been one of Tony's greatest inspirations over the years. Astaire introduced the Gershwins' standard "Fascinating Rhythm" to the world in their Broadway musical *Lady Be Good* (1924); it was the first song Tony ever recorded, in April 1949. The Gershwins wrote "They All Laughed" for the Astaire and Ginger Rogers film *Shall We Dance* (1937); Tony did a duet of the song with Lady Gaga on their 2015 GRAMMY award–winning album *Cheek to Cheek*.

"I was ten and eleven years old when those wonderful Fred Astaire and Ginger Rogers movies were first shown," Tony recalled when we talked about what shaped his desire to perform melodic and intelligent standards.

I remember as a kid seeing Astaire movies like *Top Hat, Follow the Fleet, Swing Time,* and *Shall We Dance*—movies with Fred introducing songs written by Jerome Kern, the Gershwins, Irving Berlin, and Cole Porter. He inspired them all to write some of America's best popular songs. So the "Great American Songbook" is really the Fred Astaire songbook. Years later, in the early 1970s, when I lived in Los Angeles, I got to know him as a friend and neighbor. He would stop by my home and visit with me in my art studio, and he encouraged me to continue to record these timeless songs. He reflected that "in popular music on one side is Muzak®. On the other side is this cacophonous sound. And in the center, there's a silver lining, and those songs will sustain. Tony, keep singing those songs found in the silver lining."

> " TONY BENNETT IS ONE OF THE ESSENTIAL INTERPRETERS OF THE AMERICAN SONGBOOK, MATCHING (PERHAPS SURPASSING) THE INDIVIDUAL WORLDWIDE CONTRIBUTIONS OF ELLA FITZGERALD, FRANK SINATRA, AND BING CROSBY.…HIS OFTEN SWINGING STYLE, AS WELL AS HIS PRECISE PHRASING AND IMPECCABLE TONE…, ARE ARCHETYPAL TRAITS TO WHICH SINGERS HAVE ASPIRED FOR THE PAST FIVE DECADES. "
>
> —STEVE HOLTJE AND NANCY ANN LEE, *MUSICHOUND JAZZ: THE ESSENTIAL ALBUM GUIDE,* 1998

Poster for the 1935 film Top Hat *starring Fred Astaire and Ginger Rogers, which included standards such as "Cheek to Cheek"; Astaire and his films and songs have long been some of Tony's greatest inspirations.*

Tony also attributes his affinity for recording great songs to his first music director, Tony Tamburello. Not only was Tamburello an accomplished jazz pianist and vocal coach (he would later work with, among others, Judy Garland and Juliet Prowse) but, like Tony, Tamburello was a connoisseur of the American songbook cannon. In a 1985 *New York Times* profile, critic John S. Wilson noted that "[Tamburello] seems to have at his fingertips almost every song written in the last sixty-five years." Tamburello was about six years older than Tony Bennett, and he became a wonderful friend and mentor. "He was a magnificent music teacher and played beautiful piano," Tony told me. "I was fortunate to connect with him just before I went into the recording studio because he prepared me for some of the challenges that I would face once I started making records. He had a really big personality and was very adamant when he would say to me, 'Never compromise. Only sing quality songs, only songs that are very well written. Don't do something that's just going make a big buck and then be forgotten two weeks later. Stay with quality.'"

Tamburello produced Bennett's October 1949 demo record, which contained two sides: "Boulevard of Broken Dreams," a 1933 song written by composer Harry Warren and lyricist Al Dubin; and a 1928 Irving Caesar tune, "Crazy Rhythm." The demo caught the attention of Columbia Records A&R head Mitch Miller, who, after several years of success at Mercury Records, had recently joined Columbia to record "pop" singles for the renowned label. A classically trained oboist, Miller had been lured to Columbia by one of the label's executives, Goddard Lieberson. Miller was so impressed by the demo that he signed Tony Bennett to the label in 1950. Among the artists included in Columbia's roster in the 1950s were Frank Sinatra, Duke Ellington, Benny Goodman, Dave Brubeck, Miles Davis, and Erroll Garner, as well as "new" singers like Rosemary Clooney, Frankie Laine—and now Tony Bennett.

This record unlocked the door for Tony Bennett to begin his first amazing twenty-two-year chapter with Colum-

BROOKLYN EAGLE – SUNDAY MAY 21, 1950.
BY AL SALERNO

That one break: Tony Bennett, an Astoria lad, wanted to be a singer but got only as far as a Greenwich Village club. Then one night Bob

Hope heard him. Took him to the Paramount, signed him for his next road tour and may have him in his next movie. Tony also earned a Columbia records contract. Now, at 24, he's well on the way . . .

OPPOSITE: *Mitch Miller and Tony Bennett confer on a song at a Columbia recording session at CBS 30th Street Studio, September 1957.* ABOVE: *A news clipping from the* Brooklyn Eagle, *May 21, 1950, announcing a Columbia contract for Tony Bennett, an "Astoria lad."*

bia Records, producing records that have endured many changes in popular taste yet still remain an indelible part of our popular culture—records with songs like "Strangers in Paradise," "Just in Time," "I Left My Heart in San Francisco," "I Wanna Be Around," "The Good Life," "For Once in My Life," "Maybe This Time," "Fly Me to the Moon," "The Best Is Yet to Come," "This Is All I Ask," "If I Ruled the World," and "Who Can I Turn To?" This constitutes just the short list of these classic recordings—irrefutable evidence that great songs and hit records are *not* exclusive of one another.

W ithin a year of Tony Bennett joining Columbia (a division of CBS), the company purchased a building on East 30th Street in New York City that had at one time been home to various religious congregations. Columbia had recently converted it into a recording studio, and Tony has mentioned that his first recording session in this acoustically perfect space—to record "Boulevard of Broken Dreams" on April 20, 1950—was unforgettable. "When I first recorded at the CBS 30th Street Studio [the "Church"], it was such a wonderful experience. . . . To this day, there's never been a studio better than that. And everybody from Igor Stravinsky to Leonard Bernstein, Frank Sinatra, Duke Ellington, Count Basie, Ella Fitzgerald, everybody has performed in that studio. . . . They tore it down [in the early 1980s] and to me, it was a tremendous loss. It was like someone tearing down Carnegie Hall."

Another important musical master who participated in Tony's first Columbia session was arranger Marty Manning.

Marty joined Columbia just about the same time as me. He had spent time in the 1940s arranging music for radio programs on NBC and CBS, and Mitch Miller paired us together for that first recording. If you look at the hit singles I recorded for my first chapter with Columbia you'll often see Marty Manning's name credited with arrangements. He won a GRAMMY for his work on my 1962 record of "I Left My Heart in San Francisco." That combination of Frank Laico and Marty Manning and that sacred studio space gave me such enthusiasm every time I had a recording session scheduled. I've always believed that a record is something you'll have to live with for the rest of your life, and so it's got to be perfect in every way.

> " IT'S IMPOSSIBLE TO IMAGINE THE LAST HALF-CENTURY OF AMERICAN MUSIC WITHOUT TONY BENNETT. WE'VE WATCHED YOU PREVAIL OVER REVOLUTIONARY CHANGES IN MUSIC BY EMBRACING THEM, SHAPING THEM INTO SOMETHING UNIQUELY YOUR OWN ...ALWAYS YOUR OWN! IF POST-WORLD WAR II POPULAR MUSIC HAS A VOICE, IT'S TONY BENNETT. "
>
> —ROSEMARY CLOONEY, FROM A LETTER REPRODUCED IN THE CEREMONY PROGRAM BOOKLET FOR THE SOCIETY OF SINGERS' ANNUAL ELLA AWARD, BESTOWED ON TONY BENNETT FEBRUARY 6, 2000

Sixteen songs. Tony Bennett does a quick backstage sketch of Rosemary Clooney.

Pathfinder

Gold in young voices

Singers just old enough to vote make most of today's popular record hits

By John M. Conly

"Could I get just a sandwich, Dan?" pleaded Tony Bennett. "I haven't had anything to eat since breakfast." Dan Stevens, Columbia Records' East Coast promotion manager, looked at his watch. "No," he answered heartlessly, "You're due on stage at 6:15 and it's along to make sure the nation's capital got the full impact of the Clooney-Bennett visit. At the time, Rosemary's clanging, bouncing record of Come On-a My House was moving toward the million-sales mark. Tony's Cold, Cold Heart and Because of You were just establishing semipermanent residence at the head of the country's popular best-seller lists.

When Columbia released "Boulevard of Broken Dreams" in June 1950, it brought Tony Bennett to the attention of a national radio audience, and the airplay helped lift his career off the ground. He began traveling around the country to perform at supper clubs, and he and Rosemary Clooney—another of Mitch Miller's young recording protégés—were hired as cohosts of a CBS Radio program (simulcast on CBS-TV) called *Songs for Sale*.

Tony recorded almost a dozen singles between July 1950 and January 1951 for Columbia, but nothing caught on. He recalled,

> I was getting stressed because I knew the company would not keep me on the label unless I came up with another hit. . . . Then, in July 1950, I met conductor Percy Faith. He had grown up in Toronto, came to the US in the 1940s, and had worked at Decca Records before Mitch brought him into the Columbia family. I always appreciated his low-key approach to things, and I know he sensed that I was anxious about not being able to come up with another hit. When I went to his office in early April 1951 to select a couple of songs for our recording sessions, he had a pile of sheet music on his desk. I remember him shuffling through the songs, picking one out, and handing me sheet music to a song called "Because of You." I loved the opening line, and Percy said, "When we record this just use your natural voice. With this song I see no need for any enhancement, just sing like you're having a conversation." What great advice!

The record was released in the spring of 1951, and by June "Because of You" was the number-one record in America (holding that position for approximately ten weeks) and establishing the start of a recording career that would start two centuries of unparalleled achievement and success.

OPPOSITE: Pathfinder News, *a former Washington, DC, periodical, ran this feature on Tony Bennett and Rosemary Clooney on December 12, 1951, during their week-long appearance at Loew's Capitol Theatre in DC. Tony is shown doing a quick sketch of "Rosie" backstage before a performance.* ABOVE: *Tony poses with Harry Siskind of the Master Automatic Music Company on the June 30, 1951, cover of* Cash Box, *a jukebox-industry magazine. Siskind holds boxes containing disks of Tony's best-selling hit "Because of You"; on the right, Mitch Miller of Columbia helps carry the load.*

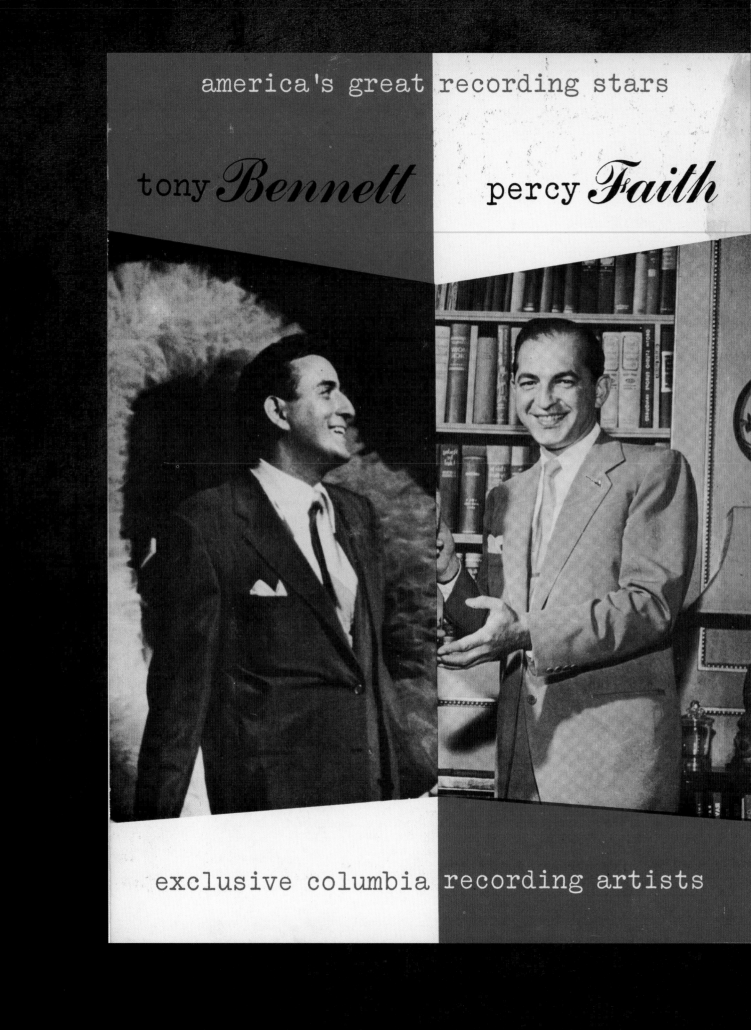

america's great recording stars

tony *Bennett*   percy *Faith*

exclusive columbia recording artists

america's great recording stars

Concert Tour
Apr. 1954

percy *Faith* tony *Bennett*

exclusive columbia recording artists

An April 1954 Columbia promo piece from a concert tour featuring Tony Bennett and conductor Percy Faith. When they recorded "Because of You," Faith advised Bennett to "use your natural voice. . . . Just sing like you're having a conversation."

Cover Subject

Tony Bennett has proved to be no flash-in-the-disc. There were many who felt that Tony wouldn't make it after *Because Of You* and *Cold, Cold Heart* had worn off. But his record sales and his personal appearance itinerary provide ample evidence that he is here to stay.

Tony just finished five weeks at the Roxy Theater in New York, where this Bob Parent cover shot was taken. And on Oct. 2 he opens at the Copacabana, his first major night club gig in the big city, for four weeks.

Billy Eckstine's Own Story (See Page 2)

★ ★ ★

Kenton Band Revitalized (See Page 2)

★ ★ ★

Johann's Bach-Log (See Page 4)

★ ★ ★

Steve Allen (See Page 2)

★ ★ ★

On The Cover Tony Bennett (See Page 1)

25 cents

Cover of Down Beat, *October 8, 1952; the cover story noted that "Tony Bennett has proved to be no flash-in-the disc. . . . His record sales and his personal appearance itinerary provide ample evidence that he is here to stay."*

"I'VE GOT RHYTHM"

Tony Bennett returned to the CBS 30th Street Studio in May 1951 for a session that would capture the artistic pattern he devised in those early "in the studio" years. The pressure to record "pop formula" songs was intense, and yet he was somehow able to navigate between recording songs that appealed to pop taste but that were also written by the composers and lyricists he so admired.

On May 31, against his personal instincts, he was convinced by Mitch Miller to record "A Cold, Cold Heart," a song written by the legendary country and western singer Hank Williams. Tony resisted: "I told Mitch that I was a 'city' boy and that he was trying to turn me into a cowboy!" Today, before Tony performs this song at a concert, he often jokes with the audience, "I told Mitch Miller he'd have to tie me to a tree to get me to record this song. And so he tied me to a tree. . . ." Tony often gets a standing ovation for this number. His 1951 record quickly became the number-one record in the country, bumping "Because of You" to number two and breaking down music genre barriers that would, going forward, help country music go mainstream. Glen Campbell, Kenny Rodgers, Willie Nelson, Patsy Cline, and dozens more gifted singer/songwriters would emerge after "Cold, Cold Heart" as radio stations across the country broadened their playlists to include country and western. Tony's connection with Nashville in the 1950s was further enhanced when, in 1956, *The Grand Ole Opry*, WSM radio's iconic Saturday evening radio show, produced a Hank Williams tribute program and invited Tony Bennett, Ray Price, and others to perform. In 2006 and 2011, when Tony Bennett went into the studio to record his hit *Duet* CD series, among the artists he collaborated with were some of the most talented singers with roots in country music, including Willie Nelson, Carrie Underwood, Tim McGraw, and Faith Hill.

Although Mitch Miller had to, as Tony stated, "tie me to a tree" to record "Cold, Cold Heart," what is revealed on the set list for the May 31, 1951, session is that Tony Bennett also recorded a beautiful standard, "While We're Young," written by his friend composer Alec Wilder. Wilder prevailed upon Miller to give Tony Bennett some freedom and latitude to choose material he was most artistically aligned with. Wilder wrote songs with great melodies and intelligent lyrics. This song is another example of a selection Tony still includes in his concerts, a timeless song to sing some sixty-seven years after he first recorded it.

Even with all his commercial recording success at twenty-six-years old, Tony had bigger goals, higher artistic ambitions. He was restless and wanted to record jazz. That day was not far away, and it would broaden the Bennett repertoire, arrangements, and choice of musicians and influence in a profound way the time he would spend in the recording studio over the next six decades.

> **"THE HOTTEST SINGER IN THE BUSINESS AS THIS IS BEING WRITTEN LIKES THE HOTTEST SORT OF MUSIC. . . . TONY HAS GREAT RESPECT FOR GREAT JAZZ MEN. . . . COLUMBIA WILL PROBABLY KEEP HIM ON THE KIND OF MATERIAL WITH WHICH HE HAS SUCCEEDED SO HANDSOMELY. BUT JUST AS THAT CRAZE STARTS TAPERING OFF, TONY'LL BE RARIN' TO JUMP ONTO THE JAZZ WAGON. . . . THERE'S NO GETTING AWAY FROM IT. . . . THIS BENNETT BOY LOVES HIS JAZZ."**
>
> —GEORGE SIMON, COVER STORY FOR *METRONOME* MAGAZINE, FEBRUARY 1952

Musicians, *sketch by Tony Bennett.*

The great success Tony had with his early recordings allowed Tony to fulfill one of his childhood dreams—to buy his mother a beautiful home. When I first met Tony's sister, Mary, she told me that these were some of her mom's most enjoyable days. Mary (who would become Tony's manager in 1955) and her husband, Tom Chiappa, moved in with her mother at the home in Bergen County, New Jersey, which became the gathering point for many memorable gatherings of family and friends.

Then in July 1951, while appearing in Cleveland, Tony met Patricia Ann Beech. They shared many of the same interests: Patricia loved jazz and painting, the two creative passions in Tony's life, and after dating for a few months, Tony proposed to her on New Year's Eve while onstage at the Paramount Theatre in New York. They married in February 1952. The couple traveled together while Tony was on the road and settled into an apartment in the New York City area until their two sons were born: D'Andrea (Danny) in 1954 and Daegal (Dae) in 1955.

Tony and Patricia eventually moved out of the city and had a beautiful Frank Lloyd Wright–style home built in Englewood, New Jersey, that would give the boys plenty of space to grow and thrive. Tony also wanted to build a recording studio in the home's basement where he could record and rehearse, and he had the great fortune to have as a friend and neighbor the highly admired recording engineer Rudy Van Gelder. Many of the most iconic records in jazz—including John Coltrane's *A Love Supreme*, Sonny Rollin's *Saxophone Colossus*, and Herbie Hancock's *Maiden Voyage*—were among the classic jazz albums recorded at the Van Gelder Studio in Englewood, not far from Tony and Pat's home. Rudy built an acoustically perfect basement studio for Tony, and as Danny and Dae grew up, they would become fascinated by music and the recording process. This would be their introduction to the world of music and recording, an experience that prepared them, years later, to professionally assist their father's career. Danny, who has managed Tony Bennett's career since 1979, told me that their childhood home was so close to Manhattan that after his dad came home from a session at the "Church," the "jam sessions would go on for hours in the basement studio." He told me,

It was very magical, but it was part of the fabric of our growing up. And when I say "basement," I'm referring to that little recording studio Tony had built down there. When my dad was on the road, you know the saying "when the cat's away, the mice will play," well, Dae and I would go down and basically pretend that we were a radio station. We'd turn the machines on and record programs with the mics. That's how we started our education, figuring out how to turn the tape machines on.

Tony and his son Dae in Englewood,
New Jersey, June 1963.

Tony Bennett and acclaimed jazz saxophonist Stan Getz, August 1964; Getz was one of the many musicians Dae and Danny got to know and learn from during the jam sessions at their father's home studio in Englewood.

Dae Bennett, a multi-GRAMMY award–winning recording engineer, also has memories of how important that home studio was to his professional life. "A lot of people discovered this area—jazz giants like Dizzy Gillespie—because of Rudy's renowned home studio in Englewood. When my parents built the Englewood house in 1956–57 it was all forest here. . . . For Danny and me, it was kind of like living in a tree house in a way because it would all open up to the outside. But the lower level is where Rudy had designed a little recording studio for Tony and had equipped it with McIntosh® amplifiers and a state-of-the-art Ampex® two-track machine. . . . That's actually what we learned on."

"As kids, Dae and I didn't know who Stan Getz was or how famous Count Basie was," Danny recalled, "but they came to our home, and sometimes we found ourselves at the piano bench with Duke Ellington, or ending up being friends with Buddy Rich."

Dae, who still plays drums, told me that when the Basie band came to the home studio, "I was very fascinated with Count Basie's drummer at the time, Sonny Payne. He was like a fireworks show going off. He was really a tremendous drummer. I was fascinated with the brushes when I was maybe eight or nine years old. . . . He took the time to show me the brushes and all that, and it was this major drum legend who actually gave me my first sticks and my first brushes. Those are the moments Danny and I talk about now, and I look back and go, 'Oh, wow. My first drumsticks are from Sonny Payne.' That's simply amazing!"

In 2012, Danny coproduced *The Zen of Bennett*, a critically acclaimed documentary that captured, in a very intimate and loving portrait, the magic of his father.

My brother and I . . . call so many of those early experiences in our lives our "Forrest Gump moments." I remember being with Tony in Washington, DC, and he was performing with Louis Armstrong and Carol Channing on the National Mall. I can also remember when JFK was running for president in 1960 and he visited Teaneck, New Jersey, to give a speech at the Teaneck Armory. He had invited Tony to be one of the guests onstage, and there I am sitting on my dad's lap behind Senator Jack Kennedy, who is giving a speech and facing that big crowd. It is those images there are frozen in my memory bank. Because I was with my father, Tony Bennett, instead of being in front of the stage, we were always at the back of the stage. So, when I did *Zen of Bennett*, it was about that point of view . . . a very close-up and inside view of Tony Bennett's life as an artist.

Director of the White House Summer Seminar, Dorothy H. Davies (back row, center), poses at the White House with Tony Bennett (far right), bassist Eugene Wright (far left), Patricia Bennett (second from right), and Dae Bennett and Danny Bennett (front), on August 29, 1962, the day after the seminar's jazz concert.

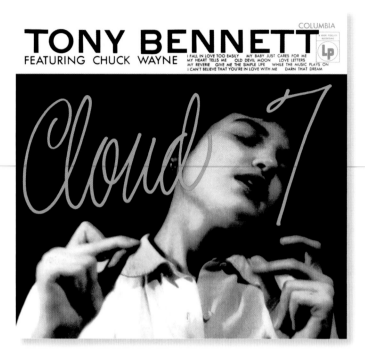

Tony Bennett has been a lifelong student, and he spent his time in those formative years as he does today, learning, absorbing, and perfecting his gifts. "By 1955, I was really restless to record a jazz-oriented album but met resistance from the label. The album format was most often reserved for classical artists or for cast albums like *South Pacific,* and the popular recording singers were confined to 45-rpm single sides," Tony remembers.

But I guess I just wore Mitch Miller down, and the company finally agreed to allow me to record my first ten-song LP, *Cloud 7*. My music director at the time, Chuck Wayne—a very gifted guitarist who had been a member of Woody Herman's band and also the first guitarist in the George Shearing Quintet—fed my ambition to pursue this project. We went into the CBS 30th Street Studio in August and December 1954 with musicians that both Chuck and I admired: Al Cohn, Ed Shaughnessy, and Gene DiNovi on piano; and for material we chose songs written by composers like Julie Styne, Walter Donaldson, Victor Young, Jimmy McHugh, Jimmy Van Heusen; and one of my favorite lyricists, Yip Harburg. It was a great experience, and fans still ask me to autograph their vinyl copies of the album!

A few years after the album was released, Tony, for the first time, met Miles Davis (who along with John Coltrane and Tony shared 1926 as their birth year). Tony told me that, "One of the songs on *Cloud 7* was something I used to sing at the Shangri-La Club in Astoria. Al Cohn was on sax, and the pianist at the club was the talented Bobby Pratt. He introduced me to the song 'While the Music Played On,' and I put it on *Cloud 7*; when I met Miles he told me that he loved that track!"

Another permanent and consistent part of Tony's "in the studio" years evolved at the beginning of his Columbia years, and that was preparation—his methodology for thor-

The cover of Cloud 7, *Tony's first ten-song LP.*

oughly rehearsing songs and being fully prepared before entering the recording studio. As Danny Bennett recalled in his impressions as a young person attending recording sessions with Tony at the CBS studio, "I don't remember the specific album he was recording or what time period it was, only that it was in the mid to late 1950s. I certainly remember sitting behind engineer Frank Laico and looking at that big orchestra and seeing Tony right in the middle of it. And just how the engineers did their thing. It was very scientific at the time, a lot of lab coats. Everyone seemed focused on the process. They ran the studios on a time clock, so you had to be fully prepared when your turn at bat came up. If you had a session that was booked between three and five, right before you would have been Bob Dylan, and right after that would be a Duke Ellington session."

Tony created a formula of preparation that has endured through the years:

When I got the opportunity to record albums with Columbia, I would spend weeks finding just the right songs. Tony Tamburello would come to my home studio with sheets of music of tunes we'd discussed. I never wanted to hear a demo record of a song because I didn't want to ever be influenced by the performance on someone else's record. I wanted to hear for myself if the song was just right for me. We'd find a key that was comfortable and take a run at it. I've always been attracted to melodies that have a very interesting harmonic pattern. If it departs from the usual chord progressions, it'll get my attention. Sometimes the thing that jumps off the sheet music for me is the lyric content. If it's just the right lyric, if I find I can identify with the story and just what the song is attempting to communicate, I will want to sing it in concert.

I also will try a song out in concert over a period of weeks to ensure that, if I'm going to record it, I've arrived at what I think is a "definitive" interpretation. I must have sang "The Shadow of Your Smile" for six weeks or more in concert before I finally felt that I'd nailed just the right approach, for me, to record the song. But all of this work has to be done before you stand in front of a mic in a recording studio.

The album cover of Tony (*later retitled* Tony Bennett Showcase*); released in 1957, it was a collection of some of the best songs from the Great American Songbook.*

Tony's next major album release was a repository of some of the best songs from the Great American Songbook. Simply titled *Tony* (later retitled *Tony Bennett Showcase*) and recorded in 1956, there are songs representing composers like Irving Berlin, Duke Ellington, and George Gershwin, with a riveting performance of Kurt Weill's "Lost in the Stars" featuring Tony singing just accompanied by guitarist Chuck Wayne for the first minute and a half.

The album included Columbia house arranger Ray Conniff, but for this project Tony also recruited arrangers with jazz backgrounds such as Gil Evans (who would be a pioneer of creating "the cool sound" in jazz with Miles Davis), Neil Hefti (who had played trumpet with Woody Herman's band in the early 1940s), and Marion Evans. Evans had worked with the Tommy Dorsey and Count Basie orchestras and would later create arrangements for Tony's 1967 album *Tony Makes It Happen*; it would be Evans who Tony would call upon years later to write the arrangement for the Bennett/Lady Gaga 2011 recording of "The Lady Is a Tramp."

A Tony Bennett sketch of Duke Ellington's orchestra.

Tony Bennett recording in the CBS 30th Street Studio, 1960.

An electrifying performance: Tony Bennett at a Columbia new talent party, New York, 1957.

Listening to this material today, it seems amazing that it ever got recorded. The commercial and marketing forces associated with record labels at that time were in flux, and popular music tastes were changing, and here was someone barely thirty years old navigating around all the institutional change to find a successful path to excellence.

While creating this body of enduring recorded work, Tony was simultaneously becoming one of the country's most successful concert performers—a unique singer (sounding only like Tony Bennett) and an electrifying performer—further connecting with his audience through radio and appearances on some of the most popular television shows. He would find a kindred musical spirit in 1957 when, while seeking a new accompanist after Chuck Wayne elected to come "off the road," pianist Ralph Sharon came into Tony's orbit. Their collaborations the 1960s and 1970s would produce recordings that earned a permanent place in the American Songbook, with twenty-five best-selling albums between 1962 and 1972.

"THE BEAT OF MY HEART"

It didn't take me too long to connect musically and personally with Ralph Sharon," said Tony when we discussed his relationship shortly after Ralph's death in the early spring of 2015. "After Chuck Wayne came off the road, the word went out that I wanted to audition musicians to assume Chuck's role with me. We arranged to use the Nola Studios in Manhattan to meet and hear some prospective candidates. The first candidate played and it was fine, but then Ralph sat down at the piano. I hadn't been fully acquainted with his past work but knew he was born in England and was only twenty years old when he was the pianist for Ted Heath's legendary English big band. He came to the United Sates in the early 1950s to pursue a professional life in jazz."

In addition to immediately enjoying Ralph's playing, when Tony first sang a number with him at Nola that day, he recognized Ralph's exceptional skill at accompaniment.

As Tony pointed out, "With all of his piano 'chops' Ralph never got in the way. He was so skillful at knowing just what note to hit and when to play it. I often felt in the studio or onstage with Ralph there was a lot of mental telepathy going on between us."

On a handshake that day, they began what would be one of the most productive and creative pairings in popular music and jazz. Sharon not only brought his formidable talent as pianist and music director to Tony's life, but he fully supported and encouraged Bennett's instincts as a jazz artist to employ the basic elements of improvisation. Ralph's jazz credentials were impressive. When he arrived in America, he started gaining traction as a pianist by working with people such as Kenny Clarke, Milt Hinton, and Jo Jones and had accompanied singers Carmen McRae, Johnny Hartman, and Chris Connor.

Tony said, "Early on, Ralph told me 'you don't want to be typecast or labeled; jazz is always about coming up with something new and inventive when you record and perform.' This is just how I had felt before I even ever walked into a recording studio. All those nights I spent visiting those clubs along 52nd Street listening to Louis, Ella, Billie Holiday, Mabel Mercer, Art Tatum, Stan Getz. These were the artists and this was the music that continues to inspire me in my life." As they began to work together, Tony's admiration for Ralph as an accompanist grew. "He knew just how to support a singer, every note he played was tasteful and correct. . . . Ralph was like a brother to me. He was so modest, but I can tell you that audiences all over the world fully appreciated his gift."

Tony Bennett and Ralph Sharon review music before a performance at Carnegie Hall, New York, June 9, 1962. The event was a legendary concert directed by Arthur Penn and Gene Saks that recorded live and released on two albums in late July 1962 as Tony Bennett at Carnegie Hall.

" [RALPH] NOT ONLY UNDERSTOOD WHAT I REQUIRED MUSICALLY BUT HE WAS SUCH A LOYAL AND SUPPORTIVE FRIEND. I'LL ALWAYS BE SO GRATEFUL HE CAME INTO MY LIFE. "

—TONY BENNETT

Ralph and Tony performed and recorded together until 1966, when Ralph wanted to stop traveling. Following in Ralph's footsteps would be other brilliant pianists/accompanists such as John Bunch and Torrie Zito, but the Bennett/Sharon magic would resume when Ralph rejoined Tony Bennett in 1979 and they continued their singular musical experience until 2007.

In Ralph, Tony had a partner who would encourage and support him on his next three jazz-influenced albums, two with Count Basie in the late 1950s and the first Tony Bennett/Ralph Sharon jazz concept album, *The Beat of My Heart*—recorded in June and October 1957 at the CBS 30th Street Studio. The concept and the premise of the project, as Ralph noted in the album's liner notes, was Tony's idea, and the foundation to the album would be the drum. "To Tony Bennett, a drum is the heartbeat of modern man, the reflection of our way of life as it is being lived today. . . . The drums were to be an integral part of the music and yet were to have their own identity and not be lost and yet they must never overshadow the voice. Some picture!"

In 1958, Tony recorded the first of a series of album sessions with the arranger and conductor Frank De Vol. This collaboration would produce three albums: *Long Ago and Far Away* (1958), *To My Wonderful One* (1960), and *Alone Together* (1961). All contained classic popular songs with arrangements by De Vol, who had started writing music when he was only twelve years old. The sessions for *Long Ago and Far Away* gave Tony his first chance to record at the Radio Recorders Studio in Hollywood. The studio was in its prime at that time, and artists like Louis Armstrong, Charlie Parker, Billie Holiday, and Mario Lanza had produced records there.

Tony Bennett's first "live" recording would be the fruition of a longtime personal goal of his, which was to perform and record with the Count Basie Orchestra. Tony first met Basie in the early 1950s when the band was performing at Birdland in New York, and there was an instant personal and professional connection. When you speak to Tony about Basie, he immediately flashes that famous Bennett smile, "Oh, he was such a wonderful and gifted human

The first Tony Bennett/Ralph Sharon jazz concept album,
The Beat of My Heart, *released in 1957.*

The recording sessions for Long Ago and Far Away, *released in 1958, were the first at the famed Radio Recorders Studio in Hollywood.*

Basie/Bennett (*later retitled* Strike Up the Band); *the album was recorded at Capitol Studios in New York, arranged by Ralph Sharon, and released in 1959.*

Basie and Bennett had been booked to appear in concert at the Latin Casino in Philadelphia; Columbia engineer Frank Laico set up his recording equipment and captured an amazing performance.

"Although some record companies were recording in stereo," Tony recalls,

> Columbia was a little behind the curve, and Frank taped the concert in monaural. Once the tapes were sent off to New York, someone at the record company said, "Oh no! We want this record in stereo, so you'll have to arrange with the band to come into the 30th Street studios and re-record the album, and we'll add an applause soundtrack." I was opposed to the idea, but a month later, during Christmas week, we recorded the sessions in New York. For years I was very unhappy with the release version with canned applause, but when my son Danny was preparing the *Complete Collection*, he and producer Didier Deutsch spent quite a bit of time tracking down our original studio session. They released a clean and wonderful version of *In Person* with me and the Basie Band. It was a thrill to hear it the way I wanted it released!"

being, and for me he was a great, great mentor. I knew that someday I hopefully would record with him." In 1958, an arrangement was made where Count Basie, under contract with Roulette Records, could record an album with Tony on Columbia if they also recorded another album that could be released on Basie's label. In November of that year,

In early January 1959, Tony reunited with the band at the Capitol Studios in New York, where Basie had recorded one of his most successful albums of the late 1950s, *The Atomic Mr. Basie*. The result was an album first entitled *Basie/Bennett* (later renamed *Strike Up the Band*).

❝ THERE WAS ALWAYS SUCH A GREAT SPIRIT IN THE STUDIO. WHEN AN ARTIST SHOWED UP EARLY FOR THEIR NUMBER, THEY WOULD STAND IN THE CONTROL BOOTH AND JUST BEAM AT WHAT THEY HEARD GOING ON IN THE STUDIO, AND THIS INSPIRED THEIR PLAYING WHEN THEIR TRACK WAS GOING TO BE RECORDED. ❞

—TONY BENNETT, ON THE RECORDING SESSIONS FOR *THE BEAT OF MY HEART*

Tony has wonderful memories of the sessions:

I loved those sessions. We did them in two nights, and, as I recall, because of our schedules, they were very late in the evening gatherings, but no one seemed tired. That band just lifted me off the ground, and it was an education just being around Bill Basie. He spoke like he played—just as every note on piano had something to say, so in conversation his words were always right on target, to the point, and filled with humor or wisdom. At that time racial prejudice was experienced by some of America's greatest musical artists. . . . I was the first white singer to ever sing with Count Basie."

"I LEARNED SO MUCH FROM BILL [BASIE] IN THOSE YEARS. EVERY NIGHT WHEN WE TOURED, I WOULD WATCH AND LISTEN VERY CLOSELY AND WHEN I HEARD BASIE COME IN ON PIANO, I SAID, "THAT'S IT. THAT's THE WAY. "HE WOULD ALWAYS CHOOSE THE RIGHT TEMPOS, THE RIGHT FEELING, AND THE RIGHT MOOD SO THAT THE PEOPLE WOULD ENJOY THEMSELVES."

—TONY BENNETT

Another time, while performing in concert with the band, Tony learned a great lesson on how humor could defuse a bigot: "There was one time after a big concert in Philadelphia with Count in a beautiful concert hall. He and I were outside just waiting for the rest of the musicians to come out and join us. Some character walked up to him and didn't recognize Basie, who was standing right next to the valet. "Get my car," the man said to Basie. Basie replied, 'I've been working all night. Get your own car.' He had a great sense of humor."

Tony Bennett is perhaps one of the most eloquent spokespersons for the unique place New York City plays in our national history. In 1996, he recorded a CD tribute to that experience, *Astoria: Portrait of the Artist* (see pages 126–127), but his first recorded musical statement on New York was released in 1959, with *Hometown, My Town*. Over three sessions at the CBS 30th Street Studio in November 1958, Tony joined arranger Ralph Burns in creating an album with full orchestral versions of songs like "Penthouse Serenade" and "The Skyscraper Blues."

"One of the things I remember most about that project was not what took place in the studio," Tony notes. "For the album cover, the photography team took me out on the Staten Island ferry. It was one of those cold and damp autumn afternoons, and I couldn't wait for them to get the photo they wanted! I was quite pleased with the results, with that beautiful skyline in the background as I looked out over New York Harbor."

Tony Bennett singing with the Count Basie Orchestra, c. 1959.

Ralph Burns and Tony Bennett working on songs for
My Heart Sings, *1961.*

Tony once again collaborated with Ralph Burns in 1961, on the album *My Heart Sings*—a tribute to some of Tony's favorite artists: Al Jolson, Sarah Vaughn, Billie Holiday, Miles Davis, Jimmy Rushing, and Mildred Bailey. By this time, Tony and Ralph had won a wide audience of jazz fans, and many of the genre's most talented players and arrangers were eager to work with them. "Jazz is America's music," Tony told me, "and its roots are in the African American experience. All of the pain and prejudice that so many of our jazz masters had to suffer never stifled their creativity; they produced a music idiom that continues to be embraced all over the world and brings great pride to the country of its origin, America." The National Endowment for the Arts established the Jazz Master Awards in the early 1980s, the highest recognition the United States can bestow upon jazz musicians and performers. In 2006, Tony Bennett's name was added to its esteemed list of honorees.

"I'VE GOT THE WORLD ON A STRING"

In 1984, several music curators at the Smithsonian identified, collected, and issued a seven-LP collection of 110 of the top American Songbook classics and the best recorded performances of those songs, entitled *American Popular Song: Six Decades of Songwriters and Singers*. Tony Bennett was represented with five definitive performances: "Sometimes I'm Happy" composed by Vincent Youmans, Alec Wilder's "I'll Be Around," Richard Rodgers and Lorenz Hart's "My Funny Valentine," and two Harold Arlen classics, "A Sleepin' Bee" and "Last Night When We Were Young."

Arlen is, in many ways, Tony's favorite composer. "He was not only a profound composer," Tony said when we did a 2005 radio tribute to Arlen, "but he was a gifted pianist and singer. I was determined to dedicate a whole album to his music, and in August 1960, Ralph and I went into the 30th Street Studio and recorded *Tony Bennett Sings a String of Harold Arlen*." Glen Osser's arrangements and

Tony Bennett Sings a String of Harold Arlen, *released in 1961, features twelve classic songs by celebrated composer Harold Arlen.*

Tony's choice of Harold Arlen classics—including "Come Rain or Come Shine," "Let's Fall in Love," and "Over the Rainbow"—resulted in a studio record that is still a thrill to listen to almost sixty years later.

"I remember when we did 'I've Got the World on a String,' the final track, on the third day of recording," Tony recalled. "The orchestra spontaneously stood and applauded! Glen, Ralph, and I were just beaming."

During our interview about Arlen, Tony expanded on just what elements of Arlen's songs appealed to him as a singer. "I think of the word *freedom* when I think of Harold's philosophy of how singers should approach his songs. He was the son of a cantor from Buffalo, and so in addition to being very influenced by jazz and the blues, Arlen's music contains some of the feelings he absorbed in the music he heard in the synagogue. . . . He encouraged you to experiment and to always just be honest when you sing his songs."

Harold Arlen and Tony Bennett at the piano, 1964.

Tony onstage a nightclub in Miami, November 1957.

The August 28, 1962, jazz concert at the President's Park in Washington, DC, for White House Summer Seminar interns. Left to right: drummer Joe Morello; bassist Eugene Wright; pianist Dave Brubeck; and Tony Bennett.

"ONE OF AMERICA'S GREAT CONTRIBUTIONS TO THE HUMAN SPIRIT IS OUR CLASSICAL AMERICAN POPULAR SONG AND AMERICA'S INDIGENOUS MUSIC, JAZZ. FOR SEVEN DECADES...TONY BENNETT HAS INTRODUCED AUDIENCES TO THIS BODY OF WORK AND TO DISCOVER THE CREATIVE GENIUS INHERENT IN THESE SONGS....HE CONTINUES TO DISTINGUISH AND HONOR OUR COUNTRY AS AN AMBASSADOR OF SONG AND HE IS A NATIONAL TREASURE."

—DR. JOHN EDWARD HASSE, CURATOR EMERITUS, DIVISION OF CULTURE AND THE ARTS, SMITHSONIAN NATIONAL MUSEUM OF AMERICAN HISTORY

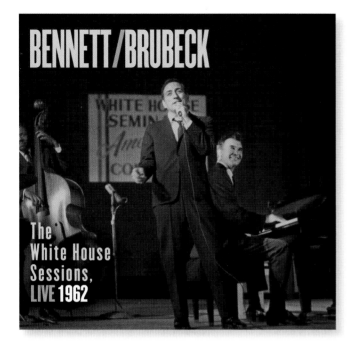

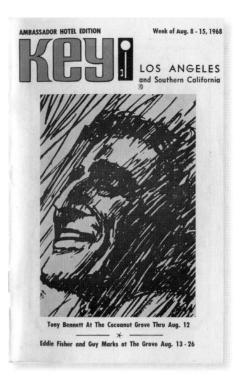

The August 28, 1962, concert in DC was recorded and later released in 2013 as a best-selling jazz CD, The White House Sessions: Live 1962.

Sketch of Tony on the cover of Key *magazine, with dates for his Cocoanut Grove appearance, Los Angeles, August 1968.*

On August 28, 1962, President John F. Kennedy invited Tony Bennett and Dave Brubeck to perform on the National Mall at the White House Seminar American Jazz Concert, organized as a way to thank several thousand students from all over the country who had served as government interns that summer. Tony and Dave were two of Columbia Records' biggest stars at the time. The plan was for Tony, Ralph, and their trio to do a set, and then Dave Brubeck's quartet would do a set. I spoke to Dave in 2010, and he told me that just before the show was to begin, President Kennedy's press secretary, Pierre Salinger, suggested to Tony and Dave that they do a couple of numbers together. They had never performed together before, but Dave told me he "jumped at the chance." The recordings of their four songs together and their individual performances were found by an astute researcher in 2012 and released in spring 2013 as *The White House Sessions: Live 1962*—quickly becoming one of the nation's best-selling jazz CDs.

With all the concert and television appearances scheduled for 1962, Tony still found time to go into the studio at least nine times that year. In July 1960, composer Cy Coleman and lyricist Carolyn Leigh (they had composed his hit single "Firefly") wrote a song with Tony Bennett in mind—"The Best Is Yet to Come." Soon after, Cy joined Tony in the studio and wrote a last-minute arrangement— and a new American standard was born. In October 1962, it was "I Wanna Be Around," and in December of that year Tony introduced "The Good Life." In April 1963, Tony recorded the definitive version of Gordon Jenkins's song "This Is All I Ask." The string of hits kept coming through the 1960s. Even with the radio dominance of rock and pop music in those years, in July 1967, you would turn on a station and frequently hear Tony's "For Once in My Life" on heavy rotation, and in February 1968, "Yesterday I Heard the Rain."

ABOVE: *Martin Scorsese and Tony Bennett pose at the Scorsese and Music Panel during the 2004 Tribeca Film Festival in New York, May 7, 2004.* **OPPOSITE:** *Tony Bennett at the CBS 30th Street Studio, September 1957.*

There's a word frequently used to describe certain performers and artists: "effortless." That's the way we used to talk about Jack Benny's routines and Johnny Carson's monologues, to name two examples. You could say the same of certain Mozart compositions for the piano, which seem to bypass musical composition and flow directly to the listener.

Of course, that's never the way it happens. The few artists who have achieved that kind of simplicity have worked hard at it. And as they work, they come to understand the beauty of silences and the slightest shifts in tone—in other words, the crucial importance of the moment, which they cultivate so carefully. One of those artists, one of the few, was born ninety years ago in Astoria, Queens. His name was Anthony Dominick Benedetto. We know him by the name Tony Bennett.

Tony Bennett recorded his first demo in 1950, and he had his first hit just a year later. The first of many. For me, and for millions and millions of others, Tony's records were woven into the fabric of life. You'd hear his voice everywhere, from passing cars or open windows across the way, from the radio in the kitchen or the record player (I still have my 78s of Tony's earliest records). It was a voice that felt warm and familiar to us, with such natural grace. And that sense of effortlessness and ease—it was there right from the start. Take "Rags to Riches," one of his many signature songs. At the beginning, the brass comes in with such a commanding sound, so big and bold, and then the voice just soars right over it, so gracefully, and quietly takes over.

So, that's seven decades of music-making—"Stranger in Paradise" in 1953, "I Wanna Be Around" and "I Left My Heart in San Francisco" in 1962, and those two extraordinary collaborations with Bill Evans in the '70s are just a few peaks along the way. And through it all, Tony's artistry has become more and more refined. It was an amazing experience to witness the renewal of his popularity in the '90s, finding his connection to new audiences by going further into the music he loved best with those three remarkable albums in a row: *Astoria: Portrait of the Artist, Perfectly Frank, and Steppin' Out.*

And now, at the age of ninety, Tony stands alone as an artist and as a human being—in his case, one in the same. His presence itself is moving, because he seems to have become one with the movement of life. That's why the title of his memoir and the film made by his beloved son, Danny, is so apt: *The Zen of Bennett.*

And on a personal note, I will say this: without Tony Bennett's music, my films and my life would have been dramatically different. His music now runs through my life like a river that never stops flowing.

> " **FOR ME, AND FOR MILLIONS OF OTHERS, TONY'S RECORDS WERE WOVEN INTO THE FABRIC OF LIFE.** "
>
> —MARTIN SCORSESE

Recording session at CBS 30th Street Studio, c.1957.

5

IN *the* RECORDING STUDIO II: 1970s–2000

"WHAT I KNOW IS, I SING THE WAY I ALWAYS SANG."

—TONY BENNETT

The singles released in the 1950s and 1960s were only a fraction of the outstanding recording output from Tony Bennett's Columbia years (see discography on pages 171–83 for a full listing). In early October 1971 and late February 1972, Tony recorded what would be his last album for Columbia (until rejoining the label in January 1986). Appropriately titled *With Love*, the album was arranged and conducted by esteemed composer/conductor Robert Farnon. In the final session at a London studio on February 26, 1972—almost twenty-two years after Tony's first Columbia single was produced—they recorded a track that would be released as a single, "Maybe This Time," which was featured in the 1972 film *Cabaret*. After completing the session, Tony and Robert went to the playback booth to listen to the results. When the record finished playing, the conductor turned to Tony and said, "That was magnificent! I bet once the public hears this, you'll have to sing this song the rest of your life!"

At this time in his career he had sold millions of records; he had won several GRAMMYs; he was continuing to create a catalogue of classic albums; he was appearing all over the world to sold-out audiences; he was guesting on popular shows and starring in his own television special; and he even had Frank Sinatra announce to the world in a 1965 *Life* magazine cover story that "for my money, Tony Bennett is the best in the business." Yet by the early 1970s, corporate culture had changed. Many artists devoted to the same music as Tony were released from record contracts, and radio stations began to abandon the music of the Great American Songbook. The British Invasion had precipitated much of this change in popular music and record sales in the United States. Ironically, Tony Bennett would begin his next chapter by moving to where it had all begun—London.

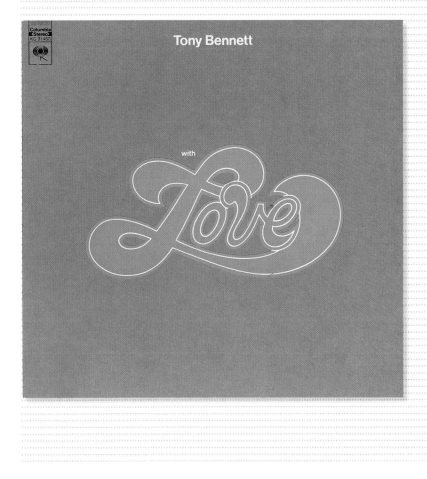

PREVIOUS PAGES: *Tony Bennett performs onstage at the Concertgebouw in Amsterdam, Netherlands, February 22, 1988.* **OPPOSITE:** *Tony Bennett at the CBS 30th Street Studio recording a song for the* Love Story *album, 1971.* **ABOVE:** *The simple but graphic album cover for* With Love, *1972, Tony's last Columbia album until he rejoined the label in January 1986.*

Tony Bennett had been visiting England since the 1950s, cultivating a loyal and growing fan base. In 1971, he signed a recording contract with MGM/Verve (the Verve label was created for Ella Fitzgerald by Norman Granz and was home to some of the iconic jazz artists). Verve maintained studios in London, and Tony moved to that city in '71, where he lived for the year with his second wife, Sandra Grant (they had two daughters, Joanna, born in 1970, and Antonia, born in 1974). One of the first projects he completed there was to record an album for his new label; once again, conductor Robert Farnon was enlisted to be Tony's musical partner. Farnon, known by many of his fellow artists as "the Governor," was also music director and conductor for the popular 1972 variety television series *Tony Bennett at the Talk of the Town*, filmed at a club located in London. "I was always inspired being around him," Tony told me. "He was revered by classical and popular artists." In October 1972, the Bennett/Farnon album *The Good Things in Life* was released by MGM/Verve, featuring the Bennett trademark mix of great songs and tasteful arrangements.

Recorded in Los Angeles and London and released in 1973, *Listen Easy* was another productive collaboration between Tony and arranger/conductor Don Costa (he had conducted the sessions on the 1965 *If I Ruled the World: Songs for the Jet Set*, which includes the original recording of the timeless Bennett classic, "If I Ruled the World").

Later in the 1970s, Tony Bennett enjoyed more major recording studio successes and produced some of his most historic recordings. Tony, along with businessman Bill Hassett, created Improv Records in 1972; during its four years of operation, the label recorded music by some great jazz giants, including Marian and Jimmy McPartland, Charlie Byrd, and Buddy Tate. One of Improv's standout releases was the 1975 album *Tony Bennett Sings . . . "Life Is Beautiful"*; its title track was the eponymous song written by Fred

Astaire. Torrie Zito arranged and conducted and Frank Laico returned as engineer. Tony and Torrie also created a Cole Porter tribute medley for the 2003 CD that contained excerpts from ten Porter songs. "For the medley, we wanted to tell a story that would contain portions of his songs. I had performed it in the summer of 1970 with Arthur Fiedler and the Boston Pops at Symphony Hall. PBS broadcast the concert, and I got a great reaction, so I had to get in down on record."

Band, sketch by Tony Bennett.

" I WAS ALWAYS INSPIRED BEING AROUND [ROBERT FARON]. HE WAS REVERED BY CLASSICAL AND POPULAR ARTISTS. "

—TONY BENNETT

LEFT: *Tony performs on* Talk of the Town, *his 1972 variety show in London with conductor and music director Robert Farnon.*

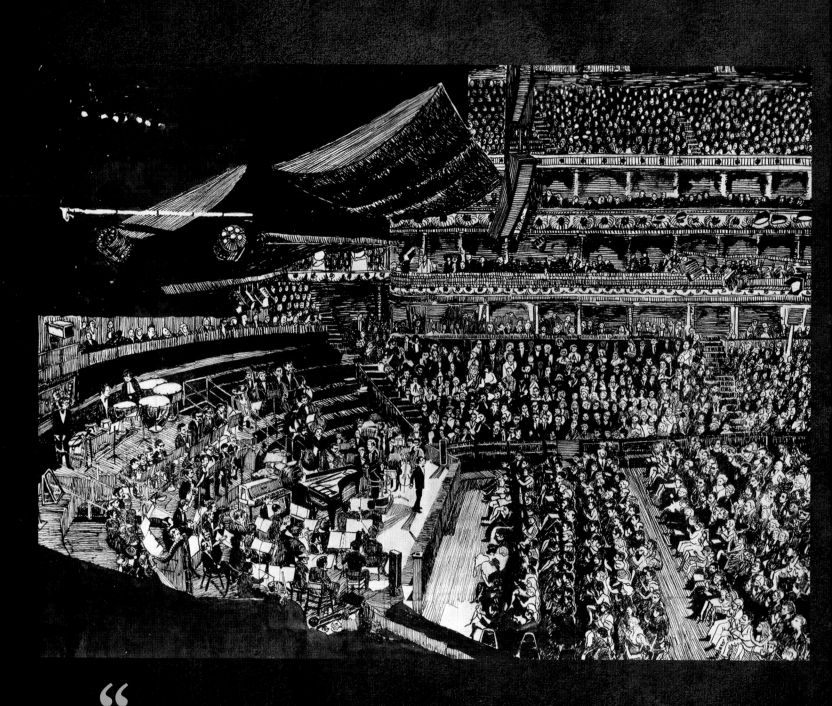

> " TED LEWIS [THE BANDLEADER] HAD TOLD ME . . .
> 'DO YOURSELF A FAVOR. PLAY ENGLAND EVERY YEAR.
> THE FANS THERE ARE UNLIKE ANY WHERE ELSE.
> THEY'RE LOYAL. **THEY NEVER FORGET YOU.**
> 'MR. LEWIS WAS RIGHT.''

—TONY BENNETT

OPPOSITE: Royal Albert Hall, *a drawing of the London concert hall by Tony Bennett, ink on paper, c. 1970s.* ABOVE: *An outtake form the photo shoot for Tony's 1971 album* Love Story. RIGHT: *Part of a Tony Bennett fan club questionnaire, 1972.* FOLLOWING PAGES: *Tony strolls through Berkeley Square, London, May 4, 1972.*

Tony produced five albums for Improv that remain at the top of jazz "must have" collections. "When I now reflect on that part of my life, I see how consistent it is with how I feel today," Tony recently said to me.

I was always trying to push forward, try new things in music, and come up with new arrangements, new songs, and new concepts. And today at ninety-one, I have the same ambitions. . . .

In the early 1970s in New York, I met Ruby Braff, the cornet player who grew up in Boston. I went to a club to hear him and his group, which included guitarists George Barnes and Wayne Wright, and John Giuffrida on bass. It was like chamber jazz, very tasteful and intimate. We talked about perhaps recording some Rodgers and Hart music.

Tony and the group started rehearsing at Lincoln Center for a July 1973 recording date at the CBS 30th Street Studio (Frank Laico engineered the session), and the wonderful results were released on two Improv LPs in September 1973: *Tony Bennett Sings 10 Rodgers & Hart Songs* and *Tony Bennett Sings More Great Rodgers & Hart*. A couple of months later, they performed the program at two critically acclaimed concerts on September 14 and 15 at Alice Tully Hall in Lincoln Center.

* * *

ANOTHER STUDIO DREAM CAME TRUE for Tony in June 1975, when he recorded the first of two voice/piano albums with Bill Evans, *The Tony Bennett Bill Evans Album,* which was released later that year. When I was producing a *GW Presents American Jazz* Bill Evans radio special in 2002, I asked Tony how those two jewels came together. "It was without question one of the highlights of my recording studio life," he said.

I'd always loved Bill's playing; his work with Miles Davis and his trio records were part of my collection. Bill and I had a mutual friend, Annie Ross, of the singing group Lambert, Hendricks & Ross. She knew Bill and suggested that perhaps he and I should record together. She then introduced us and we instantly connected. . . .

Bill said to me, "Let's leave all the cronies behind and get a studio where we can rehearse and just focus on the record." We isolated ourselves, and we came up with a list of tunes we thought would work. We spent perhaps three to four hours rehearsing to find just the right keys and the right tempos, and then Bill would put together an arrangement for each number.

When they were ready to record the album, which took place over a three-day period at Fantasy Studios in Berkeley, California, the only people present in the studio were the two artists, Bill Evans's manager, Helen Keane, and the engineer Don Cody.

A year later, in the summer of the country's bicentennial and just a few months before recording their second album, the two masters headlined the 1976 Newport Jazz Festival with a Carnegie Hall concert in June. That week Tony had agreed to a request from WNEW radio host William B. Williams to be a guest on a public affairs program Williams hosted for the US Army. As they were closing one of the segments, Williams asked Bill if he characterized Tony's music as jazz. Evans replied, "As far as I'm concerned it is. Occasionally fans will act surprised by the fact Tony and I have joined together for this particular project, because they tend to see Tony in the superstar pop singer image. But you know, every great jazz musician I know idolizes Tony. From Philly Joe Jones to Miles Davis, you name it. The reason is that Tony is a great musical artist. He puts music first and has dedicated himself to it. He has great respect for music and musicians, and this comes through, and it's just a joy to work with somebody like that. . . . This is one of the prime experiences of my life."

"HE WAS A BIG GUY BUT SPOKE SOFTLY AND WITH SUCH INTELLIGENCE. WE AGREED ON SO MANY THINGS, NOT JUST MUSICALLY—WE SHARED SIMILAR VIEWS ON ARTISTIC CREATIVITY AND ABOUT HUMANITY."

—TONY BENNETT ON BILL EVANS

Bill Evans and Tony Bennett work on The Tony Bennett Bill Evans Album, *1972.*

In late September 1976, Bennett and Evans spent two days at the Columbia Studios in San Francisco recording what would be another masterpiece—*Together Again*, released in 1977. One of the highlights is "You Must Believe in Spring," with music by Michel Legrand and English lyrics by Alan and Marilyn Bergman (the original French lyrics were by Jacques Demy). In the liner notes to the 2003 CD, the Bergmans wrote: "When you write a song, it's because you have something you want to say. When you finish it, you hope you've said what you meant. When you hear it sung, there are those magical rare times when it's what you meant and more. When we heard Tony and Bill's interpretation of 'You Must Believe in Spring,' we knew it was one of those times." This is the same insight Sinatra shared about Tony in 1965: "[Tony] gets across what the composer had in mind and probably a little more."

The second standout track is "A Child Is Born," with music by Thad Jones accompanied by poetic lyrics that were added by Tony's friend, the composer Alec Wilder. "Tony performs 'A Child Is Born' with special tenderness," wrote Wilder in the liner notes. "He gives to each word a verbal image, extremely sensitive respect, and lovingness. He sings the lovely melody with piano accompaniment only, which is all that is needed, since it is in the phenomenally talented hands of Bill Evans."

Tony mused during our 2002 Bill Evans radio tribute interview, "It's been over forty years since we made those records, and I've discovered that the appreciation for them

Bill Evans, *portrait*
by Tony Bennett,
ink on paper.

continues to grow. It proves to me something the actor Donald O'Connor told me when I lived in Hollywood: 'It always takes at least five years after you create something that is classic to be generally recognized by the public as something exceptional.' And that's been the case with those two Bill Evans albums."

"PICK YOURSELF UP"

In April 1977, Carl Jefferson, founder of independent jazz label Concord Records—based just outside San Francisco—invited Tony to contribute two tracks to what would be a nine-track LP of Duke Ellington songs titled *A Tribute to Duke*. Tony contributed "Prelude to a Kiss" and "I'm Just a Lucky So and So"; he

is accompanied by pianist Nat Pierce. Other performers on the LP include Rosemary Clooney, Woody Herman, and Bing Crosby, and the album cover features a watercolor portrait of Duke Ellington painted by Tony.

Even without a record-label affiliation during this period of his career, Tony continued to perform around the world, appear on television, and consistently get rave reviews. But in the late 1970s there was turbulence in his life outside "the studio."

"I have never lost a passion to sing and to paint," he told me, "but at that time, my personal life was in chaos. I was going through a very painful divorce that would separate me from my two beautiful daughters, and my mother died in 1977; to cope, I began to cultivate a less disciplined personal life and got in trouble. It was just a dark time for me, and I lost my balance." That's when Tony recalled a

Tony poses in front of the Golden Gate Bridge, 1976.

discussion he had with his friend, drummer Buddy Rich. "Buddy really helped me open my eyes to what I had to do. 'Tony,' he said, 'there is a very popular adage in show business that everyone seems to repeat over and over—"remember, you're only as good as your last performance!" Well I think this is completely the wrong way to approach things. The real truth is you're only as good as your *next* performance; you should have learned something from your *last* show that you can improve and then make the next one better.' And, he told me, this applies to both our personal and professional lives." That conversation became "a moment of truth" that helped to give Tony the impetus to, as the Jerome Kern song with lyrics by Dorothy Fields says, "pick yourself up, dust yourself off, and start all over again."

One of the anchors in Tony's life was his children. His two young daughters were blossoming, and for two decades, he had watched with pride as his two older sons, Danny and Dae, had developed their passion for music. Soon after the conversation with Buddy Rich, Tony called his sons and asked that they meet with him to discuss the future.

"In addition to their professional skills," Tony said he admired something else about Danny and Dae. "I was really proud of the personal values they demonstrated. They were hard workers and very disciplined about their business and were gaining quite a good reputation for their producing and engineering work. I knew they would be honest in any evaluation of my professional life and that they would have some intelligent ideas and concepts for me to consider." Tony invited his sons out to California for an initial exploratory meeting. Dae listened but ultimately stepped back; he felt Danny had more of the skill set that would best serve Tony at that time: "I read a book once that concluded that there are two kinds of people: hunters and farmers. And that describes Danny and me. He's the hunter; I'm the farmer. I understood it was probably not the best career move of my life, but you have to go with what your gut's telling you, and I knew I was already

gravitating more toward the recording business that I was starting." (Dae would later become a part of the dynamic Bennett team after Tony returned to the recording studio.)

Danny and Tony worked together for several years developing strategies to reach new audiences that, Danny fully believed, would be dazzled—as audiences had been for thirty years—by a Tony Bennett performance. Tony's sister, Mary, who at one time managed her brother's business affairs, told me that "the most consistent ambition for Tony has always been to try and create opportunities for young audiences to be exposed to the classic American songs and to jazz."

" WHEN I SPOKE WITH DANNY, I KNEW HE UNDERSTOOD MY GOALS. HE KNEW I WASN'T GOING TO CHANGE MY REPERTOIRE OR MY STYLE OF PERFORMING. YOU CANNOT FOOL AUDIENCES. YOU CAN'T FAKE SINCERITY OR BE PATRONIZING TO AN AUDIENCE, AND HE KNEW AND UNDERSTOOD THAT ABOUT ME. "

—TONY BENNETT

As of this writing, Tony and Danny's professional relationship is almost going on forty years, and it has produced legendary results. In a conversation I had with Danny recently, he pointed out that his initial professional relationship with Tony was like a jazz performance, and it began like an improvised solo. "It wasn't concrete," he told me,

it evolved, and it evolved very much like writing a song or creating a painting. I can't separate those things out. It's being methodical and creative at the same time. In my recent new role as president of Verve Records, I feel like I'm painting, I'm creating. I like sketching, I like building foundations, and I like—this is Tony's line—"meeting opportunity with preparedness," and that's all we do. We talked about his career goals and ambitions, and we came up with a pathway that would lead us there. It's like that adage where the plane is flying, and they're in the clouds, and it looks like they're going to crash land. There's a wise man on board, and he goes to the pilot, and he says, "You're reading the controls, not the clouds." That's the philosophy that I grew up with. So, you're meeting opportunity with preparedness—you're not faking it, but you're looking for those doorways, and sometimes, you have five wonderful options, so your chance of success is actually greater.

Danny also understood that his father's success was built on a foundation of artistic integrity, "Something I learned from Tony and heard Quincy Jones say recently . . . when he was asked in an interview about commercialism in music, he replied that if you only think about fame and money, then 'God walks out of the room.'

Jazz, *sketch by Tony Bennett.*

"Tony and I agreed from the very start that in promoting records or concerts, it's our job to make sure that we capture the imagination of the public. That's our job as marketers. It's not toothpaste we're trying to promote. With Tony Bennett we're promoting someone who brings to his audience—through his music—hopes and dreams. It's not about money. It's not about sales. It's about people putting their hopes and dreams in our hands."

Danny was convinced that young audiences would respond in such a positive way to Tony and to the music he represented, explaining, "I told Tony that I thought college kids are really going to connect with him because what he does, what Tony Bennett represents in our culture, transcends demographics. For young people not to have the opportunity to see and hear him was a sin. It's a sin. You wouldn't tell your eight-year-old not to go look at a van Gogh or David Hockney painting, would you? But the culture was saying you can't listen to the music of Tony or Sinatra or Ella. And I believed that was ridiculous."

This led Danny to devise ways to get exposure for Tony in front of younger audiences, and to do it in a way that Tony would remain Tony, singing only the songs he loved with absolutely no artistic compromises.

I've always enjoyed reading history, and when Tony and I would sit down to talk at that time, it had the air of planning a presidential campaign. One day during this time, I read an article on Bob Guccione Jr., who was the editor of *Spin* magazine. *Spin* interviewed him about who he thought were the most influential people in rock and roll, and he said, "Chuck Berry and Tony Bennett." I was like, "What?" So, I just called him up. He grew up in Tenafly, New Jersey, next door to Englewood. We became fast friends, and he told me, "Listen, what Tony Bennett does with music"—and this is where I came up with the phrase that "Tony never sings the same thing *once*"—"he's always taking chances. He's always looking. He's on a musical journey." I asked him

if there was something we could do with Tony and *Spin*, and he says, "Well, we have a fashion issue coming up, which we do every year. Why don't we do something with Tony and the Red Hot Chili Peppers?"

> " **WE DID A FASHION SPREAD WITH THE RED HOT CHILI PEPPERS IN LOS ANGELES, AND THAT WAS KIND OF THE FIRST THING, AND THAT JUST GOT PEOPLE'S IMAGINATION GOING.** "
>
> —DANNY BENNETT

Another significant event for Tony at this time was reconnecting with Ralph Sharon. In 1966, Ralph had left the road to spend time with his family. When Torrie Zito—who had done wonderful work with Tony as his music director and conductor—decided in the late 1970s that he wanted to stop touring, Tony reached out to Ralph, who was eager to pick up their musical collaboration where they'd left off. "I was very pleased," Tony told me, and "it felt wonderful to be working with him again. Before too long we added Bill Evans's great drummer Joe LaBarbera, and Paul Langosch on bass. They all sounded terrific every night! We got a great reaction when we played Carnegie Hall in May 1981. And the following year, I had another memorable experience when I was invited to record a ninety-minute PBS special in Boston that featured me and my group with Count Basie and his orchestra in a concert taped at the Berklee College of Music. The second half of the special featured me and pianist Dave McKenna performing together at the Copley Plaza Hotel in Boston. . . . He was such a great player."

LEFT: Ralph Sharon, *oil on canvas portrait by Tony Bennett.* ABOVE: *Tony Bennett poses with Flea (left) and Anthony Kiedis of the Red Hot Chili Peppers at the 1993 MTV Video Music Awards in Los Angeles, September 2, 1993.*

> "I ONCE ASKED COUNT BASIE WHAT I SHOULD DO. SOME OF MY FRIENDS WERE TRYING TO SING ROCK, AND I DIDN'T KNOW WHAT TO DO. BASIE TOLD ME IN THAT SLY, WISE WAY OF HIS, 'WHY CHANGE AN APPLE?'"
>
> —TONY BENNETT

Tony performs on the ABC-TV variety show Saturday Night Live with Howard Cosell, *November 22, 1975.*

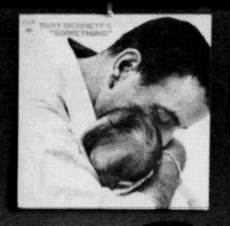

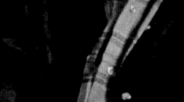
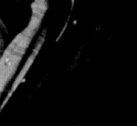
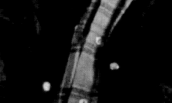

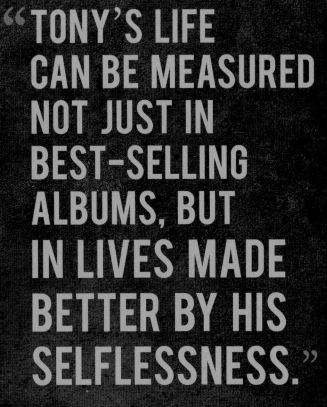

"TONY'S LIFE CAN BE MEASURED NOT JUST IN BEST-SELLING ALBUMS, BUT IN LIVES MADE BETTER BY HIS SELFLESSNESS."

—PRESIDENT BILL CLINTON

Tony surrounded by some of his best-selling albums, 1978.

Another platform the Bennetts explored was television. In 1982, Danny arranged for his father to make a guest appearance on the hip Canadian sketch show *SCTV*—which featured rising comics such as John Candy, Eugene Levy, Martin Short, and Andrea Martin. Tony appeared numerous times on *The Tonight Show* in the 1980s, and the *Simpsons* producers called in 1990. "I liked the *Simpsons*," Danny said,

and it was just getting started on Fox. They were building a loyal audience of young viewers, the same audience I wanted to see Tony Bennett. They wanted Tony to sing a song on one of the episodes. I said to him, "Look, I really like this show, and it's really weird, but I think it could be fun for you to be a cartoon character on it. This guy Matt Groening, who created the show—which is gaining a cult following with college kids—is calling, and maybe if I can convince him to have you as a character, I'd love that." Tony said, "OK, we'll do it, and let's see what happens." And so, Tony was the first character to appear as himself on the show, and he sang "Capitol City."

The game plan was beginning to work; a whole new generation was discovering a national treasure. "All of a sudden," reflects Danny, "I was playing college shows with Tony and positioning him as alternative music. So, people like Nirvana and Pearl Jam and the Chili Peppers, they were embracing Tony as the alternative and for what he has always been, 'the real thing.'"

I witnessed the success of this approach in spring 1992, when Tony Bennett and composer Michel Legrand (on piano) performed with the Boston Pops at Symphony Hall, conducted by John Williams. Tony had invited me to the concert (which was broadcast by PBS) and added, "Danny has put together an appearance the night before the concert at the Boston Hard Rock Cafe. It should be fun."

The event was sponsored by the top alternative rock radio station in Boston at the time, the legendary WBCN—"The Rock of Boston." They had added Tony's music to their playlist in 1986, as Tony was gaining fans with young people. As I looked around the crowded room that evening, I thought, not only is Tony successfully connecting with a new audience, but I recognized faces in the crowd who might not have been at the Hard Rock unless Tony was there: Harry Ellis Dickson, associate conductor of the Boston Pops; the Boston Celtics legend Tommy Heinsohn, and Michel Legrand. Ralph Sharon and the group were in place onstage, and when Tony walked in with Danny, the room exploded with applause. The station's promotions director Cha-Chi Loprete introduced Tony, who did a six-song set. There was such a strong applause for each number that I didn't think the audience would let him stop that night. The same thing happened the next evening at Symphony Hall with the Boston Pops audience, demonstrating why Tony is beyond category.

Things were perfectly aligned in Tony's life at this point for him to return to one of the most enriching aspects of his professional life: he was ready to go back into the recording studio.

OPPOSITE: *A cel of Tony Bennett's character from* The Simpsons—*the first character to appear as himself on the show. The cel is inscribed by show creator Matt Groening with a note of thanks from him and Bart Simpson. "Dancin' Homer," the episode with Tony's character, aired on November 8, 1990.*

"SHAKING THE BLUES AWAY"

In addition to building new audiences in the 1980s, Tony Bennett's personal life changed when he met Susan Crow. She had grown up in the San Francisco area, had come east and attended Fordham University, and graduated from Columbia. She not only loved jazz, but she also loved teaching and joined the faculty of the Fiorello H. LaGuardia High School of Music & Art and Performing Arts to teach social studies. They married in 2007. She and Tony both share a passion for arts education, and in 1999 they founded Exploring the Arts, an organization whose mission is to assist in subsidizing arts education programs in public schools. Two years later they established the Frank Sinatra School of the Arts (see page 24). In 2015, they were awarded the George Washington University President's Medal for their work.

With Tony's encouragement, Danny continued talking with record companies and in 1985, Tony rejoined Columbia Records. In addition to any new recordings he would produce, being back on the label would give Danny and Tony some control of reissues from his catalogue onto the then-new compact disc (CD) format.

In early 1986, Tony began the first recording sessions for *The Art of Excellence* album in London at Olympic Sound Studios. The Ralph Sharon Trio joined conductor/arranger

Jorge Calandrelli and Tony to create an album that lived up to its title in every way. One of the highlights is a selection that still never fails to produce a standing ovation when performed at one of Tony's concerts: "How Do You Keep the Music Playing?" The album cover features a striking photo taken by Annie Leibovitz. As Danny explained, "She did all the covers of *Rolling Stone*. We both worked very hard together and came up with the idea of having Tony photographed on the other side of the river, and she put him up against the World Trade Center towers. He had that big Benetton *B* on his sweater.

"With *The Art of Excellence*, we used the highest recording technology at the time, digital technology. It was an all-digital record from an artist who first began recording halfway through the twentieth century on the analog format and whose first records were issued on vinyl 78 rpms."

* * *

OPPOSITE: *Tony Bennett and Susan Crow in front of the Golden Gate Bridge, San Francisco, 1990s.* ABOVE: *Tony and Susan attend a gala for their foundation, Exploring the Arts, at Cipriani, New York, September 27, 2015.* RIGHT: Ralph Sharon and Jon Burr, *ink on paper drawing by Tony Bennett. Burr was a bassist in the Ralph Sharon trio.*

Recording session with Ray Charles at Larabee Studios in Los Angeles, January 1986, for their duet on Tony's LP The Art of Excellence, *released in May of that year by Columbia.*

THE TONY BENNETT/DUETS CONCEPT had a very auspicious start when, for *The Art of Excellence*, Danny and Dae suggested to Tony that he record a duet with Ray Charles. The two artists had never performed together, but neither had to be convinced that it would great fun to sing a duet of the James Taylor song "Everybody Has the Blues." The album was released in May 1986. At age sixty, Tony Ben-

nett had begun a new and unprecedented recording chapter that would produce best-selling hit records, GRAMMY Awards, and Emmy-winning television specials. New generations of listeners would be exposed to and embrace the classic American standards, and Tony would garner a worldwide audience of millions of new fans.

Tony signs the program poster for the Irving Berlin Centennial birthday tribute concert at Carnegie Hall, New York, May 11, 1988.

"
GOD BLESS IRVING BERLIN; HE'S THE HEART AND SOUL OF AMERICAN SONG."

—TONY BENNETT

I n May 1987, father and sons would collaborate on Tony's CD tribute to composer Irving Berlin. Danny produced the album *Bennett/Berlin*, which was recorded at Dae's Hillside Studios in Englewood, New Jersey; as always, the music content was the starting point from which everything would flow. The country, and indeed the world, was preparing for the celebration of composer Irving Berlin's centennial, and it was an occasion to reflect on the extraordinary role his music had played in twentieth-century America. Tony invited some of his favorite jazz artists to participate and do some guest solo work: George Benson on guitar; Dexter Gordon on sax; and on trumpet, Dizzy Gillespie. As Dae recalled, "Dizzy lived in the area and came in and played on 'The Song Is Ended' and on 'Russian Lullaby.' I remember on that track Ralph Sharon said, 'Well, why don't you just play thirty-two bars, and they'll edit it down to whatever?' Dizzy replied, 'Thirty-two bars? Then I'm going have to play everything I know.' He was a great guy."

On the back cover of the album is a note from Tony: "God Bless Irving Berlin; he's the heart and soul of American song." The album was released in November 1987; six months later, on May 11, 1988, Tony was invited to perform at the Irving Berlin Centennial birthday concert at Carnegie Hall. Among others, Frank Sinatra, Ray Charles, Walter Cronkite, Rosemary Clooney, Bob Hope, Willie Nelson, Joe Williams, Isaac Stern, and Natalie Cole were onstage to pay tribute to Mr. Berlin. Accompanied by some stellar brushwork from drummer Joe LaBarbera, Tony sang an Irving Berlin song written in 1927, the year after Tony was born: "Shaking the Blues Away."

In 1991, Tony Bennett released a Columbia Records four-CD, eighty-seven-track collection entitled *Forty Years: The Artistry of Tony Bennett*. Danny Bennett was executive producer and Dae Bennett was involved in the digital remixing of some of the masterful performances captured at Columbia from April 1950 through May 1989. The dedication written by Tony for the liner notes gives an insight into his sense of personal and artistic contentment at this time in his life, and reflects his sense of gratitude—a value that has always informed his music and his painting:

> This collection is dedicated to my mother and to Ralph Sharon, Tony Tamburello (my singing coach), Gian Carlo Menotti, Alec Wilder, Mabel Mercer, Duke Ellington, Frank Sinatra (who taught me not to compromise, and to sing only the best popular songs), Frank Laico (my favorite longtime audio engineer), and to my son Danny, who has managed me for years and made it possible for me to sing what my mind and heart told me.

In spring 1989, Tony went back to his roots, recording *Astoria: Portrait of the Artist*. Produced by Danny with arrangements written by Jorge Calandrelli, the album was recorded in Astoria at the renowned Master Sound Astoria studios and released in February 1990.

Danny suggested that the CD imagery convey just how much that experience still resonated in Tony's life: the front cover features a black-and-white photo of a sixteen-year old Anthony Benedetto standing in front of his childhood home; the back cover depicts sixty-three-year old Tony Bennett standing in front of that same home.

Some of the song titles capture the essence of this musical autobiography: "A Little Street Where Old Friends Meet," "It's Like Reaching for the Moon," "I Was Lost, I Was Drifting," and three new compositions written at Tony's request by composer Charles DeForest specially for the project—"Where Do You Go From Love," "I've Come Home Again," and "When Do the Bells Ring for Me?" Tony added the latter track to his concerts, where it would bring the house down. On Sunday, January 17, 1993, he gave a powerful performance of the song on the steps of the Lincoln Memorial as part of Bill Clinton's 1993 presidential inaugural celebration.

> "I CONSIDER MYSELF EXTREMELY FORTUNATE TO BE ENTERING MY FOURTH DECADE AS A PERFORMER. THE FURTHER I MOVE AHEAD THE MORE I LEARN TO APPRECIATE THE FOUNDATION I HAD AS A KID GROWING UP IN SUCH A UNIQUE AND WONDERFUL ENVIRONMENT. I WAS A KID IN PURSUIT OF THAT OFTEN-ELUSIVE 'AMERICAN DREAM,' WITH A BURNING DESIRE TO MAKE IT IN THE BIG CITY. IT JUST GOES TO SHOW YOU HOW FAR A LITTLE FAITH IN ONESELF CAN GO."
>
> —TONY BENNETT, DEDICATION ON THE LINER NOTES TO *ASTORIA: PORTRAIT OF THE ARTIST*

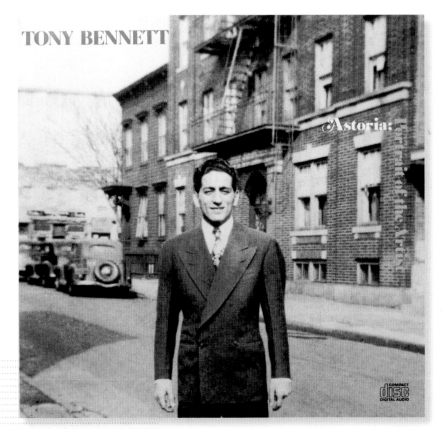

The front cover of Tony's seminal 1989 album, Astoria: Portrait of the Artist, *shows him as a young man in 1942 standing on the street where he grew up in Astoria, Queens.*

In the back cover photograph of the album, Tony stands on the same street in 1989.

Tony and Frank after their duet on Frank's show,
Sinatra and Friends, *which aired on April 21, 1977.*

Tony dedicated his performance to the names etched on the wall at the nearby Vietnam Veterans Memorial. Danny talked about the impact of album after it was released:

All of a sudden, he gets nominated for a GRAMMY. He didn't win that year, but how he won was he got that two-minute standing ovation for his live nationally broadcast performance of "When Will the Bells Ring for Me?" What a way to be introduced to a new audience and be reintroduced to your core audience. It's funny but at first [the GRAMMY committee] didn't know what category Tony's albums should be in. *Astoria* was nominated in the Best Jazz Vocal Album category. They came up with a new one in 1992—Best Traditional Pop Vocal Album—and the rest is history. Tony's won it every time he's been nominated in that category, so I don't know if they regret it or not. Perhaps they should call it the Tony Bennett category!

In early 1992, Tony Bennett and Ralph Sharon conceived of a tribute to Frank Sinatra, and in June of that year they recorded *Perfectly Frank*. "He was one of my great teachers," Tony told me when the album was released. "It's funny but I would sometimes read that there was a competitive game going on between us and I smiled because that was so far from the truth. We were both in the same business of performing and recording great songs, so I think we inspired each other. He was a decade older than me; when I was sixteen Sinatra left Tommy Dorsey and started out as a solo act. I remember going to the Paramount Theatre in Manhattan in those years and how he caused riots when he appeared—the young people were so eager to get in and see him perform. Later, when I began my career, I got to meet him and that began a decades-long friendship."

Instead of including some of the more obvious Sinatra hits like "Witchcraft," "Nice and Easy," or "Summer Wind," Tony wanted to record songs associated with Sinatra that became standards because of the Sinatra magic. "Last Night When We Were Young," "You Go to My Head," and "I Fall in Love Too Easily" were among the standout tracks. Danny told me, "In his tribute, Tony wanted to capture Sinatra's great ears for choosing great songs to sing. It gave [Tony] credibility and well-deserved appreciation because he wasn't just taking the easy path. He never takes the easy path—and that's what gave him the credibility." When the envelope was opened at the 1993 GRAMMY Awards show, *Perfectly Frank* won Best Traditional Pop Vocal Album.

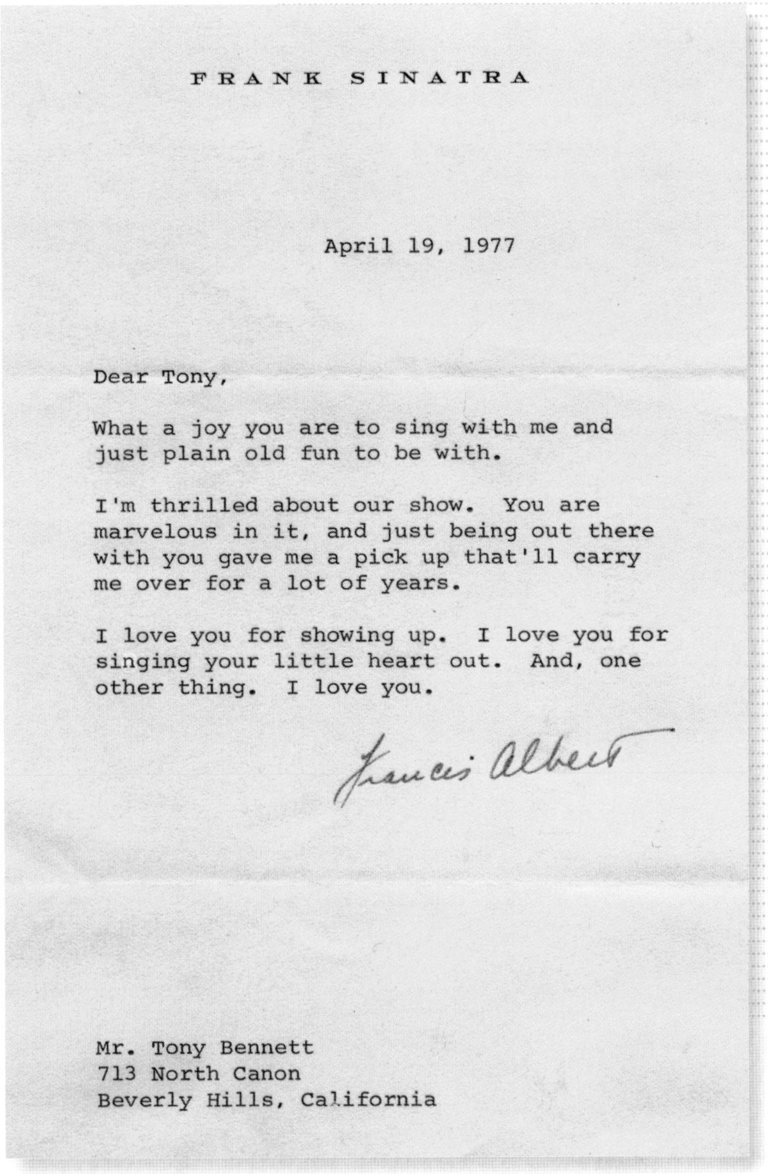

* * *

FRANK SINATRA

April 19, 1977

Dear Tony,

What a joy you are to sing with me and just plain old fun to be with.

I'm thrilled about our show. You are marvelous in it, and just being out there with you gave me a pick up that'll carry me over for a lot of years.

I love you for showing up. I love you for singing your little heart out. And, one other thing. I love you.

Francis Albert

Mr. Tony Bennett
713 North Canon
Beverly Hills, California

An April 19, 1977, letter from Frank Sinatra to Tony Bennett, thanking Tony for appearing on Sinatra and Friends.

"SINATRA WOULD COUNSEL ME TO JUST KEEPING SINGING THE GREAT SONGS I RECORDED AND THE REST WOULD TAKE CARE OF ITSELF."
—TONY BENNETT

ABOVE: *The cover of* Steppin' Out, *released by Columbia in October 1993, and which won the 1993 GRAMMY Award for Best Traditional Pop Vocal Performance.* LEFT: *The GRAMMY card announcing the 1993 win for* Steppin' Out.

Perhaps there was no better way to pay tribute to the timelessness of the American Songbook standards than by recording an album dedicated to the genius of Fred Astaire. Many people associate Fred Astaire with the brilliant dancing routines he and Ginger Rogers created and performed together onscreen, but to Tony and countless others, it was the songs Fred introduced and sang in those classic films that made an indelible impression. "The joy I had in recording the Astaire tribute album *Steppin' Out* was the abundance of great songs to pick from," Tony said to me when we did a Fred Astaire birthday tribute radio program in 2006.

"The Gershwins, Irving Berlin, Cole Porter—they produced some of their most enduring songs for Fred to sing in films. In the early 1950s, Norman Granz at Verve Records got Fred to go into the recording studio with pianist Oscar Peterson and the Jazz at the Philharmonic All-Stars. Fred revisited many of the songs he first introduced, but this time with a jazz background and better fidelity, and to this day I still listen to those records."

In summer 1993, Tony and the Ralph Sharon Trio, now with Doug Richeson on bass and Clayton Cameron on drums, went into the Clinton Recording Studios in New York City—where Miles Davis, Herbie Hancock, and Paul Simon had all made records—to record eighteen tracks of some of America's most familiar songs, including Berlin's "Change Partners," Porter's "I Concentrate on You," and the Gershwin brothers' "They All Laughed." The record won the GRAMMY in 1994 for Best Traditional Pop Vocal Album.

The hottest television platform for popular music in 1993 was MTV, so Tony and Danny pitched the concept of creating a video of Tony performing the album's title tune, Berlin's "Steppin' Out with My Baby"—sung by Astaire in the 1948 film *Easter Parade*—and having it added to the MTV "Buzz Bin," the channel's influential rotation of buzzworthy new music videos. When it first aired, it created

such enthusiasm that MTV management wanted to meet with Tony, Danny, and Columbia to discuss the possibility of a Tony Bennett *MTV Unplugged* special. Danny's recollection of that important moment reveals how single-minded he and his father were about always leading with quality songs, without compromise.

The group of us were gathered around a big conference table. . . . They were saying that a Tony Bennett special would be fantastic! They would have Tony sing songs written by various rock and pop bands while onstage with those bands. I stood up and said, "You know what, guys? I'm out." And they're like, "What are you talking about?" and I said, "Listen, I'm sorry. I'm just not interested," and I walked out of the meeting. The record label guy followed me and began just freaking out. I said, "Just wait a second. I have a strategy here." "You can't just walk out of a meeting with MTV!" he yelled, and I said, "Well, no, and you're going to pull me back in the meeting, dude. So, pull me back in."

We walked back to the conference room, and their jaws were dropped because I was throwing away this crazy and, from their view, amazing opportunity. So I said, "What would really be new and cutting edge for MTV is if you made these artists sing *Tony's* songs and let Tony do what *he* does." And then, they got it, and that was that."

The *MTV Unplugged* concert took place on April 12, 1994, at the Sony Music Studios in New York, before a highly charged studio audience. Tony and the Ralph Sharon Trio—with guests k.d. lang (on "Moonglow") and Elvis Costello (on "They Can't Take That Away from Me")—performed an evening of unforgettable performances. The soundtrack of the TV special was released as a CD that June; it would receive the GRAMMY for Record of the Year in 1995 and a second GRAMMY for Best Traditional Pop Vocal Album.

In his autobiography *The Good Life*, Tony talked about his joy on GRAMMY night:

> I can't describe how elated I felt when they opened the envelope and said, "and the winner is . . . Tony Bennett." The audience jumped to their feet, and Danny and I gave each other a knowing look that made it clear that we were not the only ones who truly knew how much this night meant. I was so proud that I invited Danny to join me onstage. To say it was a personal triumph would be an understatement: it was the culmination of everything I had been working toward for the last fifteen years, and it exemplified everything I had dreamed of accomplishing thirty years before that.

Danny, remembering that night, told me, "When we won Album of the Year and the CD was one of the year's biggest-selling records, to me, that's the triumph of it—not the award, but that's the triumph. What I cared about was that the industry and our peers recognized the need to have real music before the public, and that made a huge statement and that was the triumph as far as I'm concerned."

The following year, Tony and Danny created a concept for an interactive television format for the A&E Network called *Live by Request*. On Valentine's Day 1996, Tony starred in the first in a series of live shows in which viewers would request songs by phone or email for singers or bands to perform on air. Tony's episode was a hit, with more than 1.5 million viewers calling in to request songs. "That was my foray into television and producing television shows," Danny said. "It was very exciting because, again, we were doing things early on that nobody else was doing. Live television had literally disappeared—it's a high-wire act." The show won the Emmy Award that year for Individual Performance in a Variety or Music Program and would also earn the coveted CableACE Award.

BELOW, LEFT: The soundtrack to Tony's April 12, 1994, appearance on MTV Unplugged was released in June of that year, and went on to win two GRAMMYs: Album of the Year and Best Traditional Pop Vocal Performance. BELOW, RIGHT: Close-up of the GRAMMY for Album of the Year for MTV Unplugged. OPPOSITE: Tony Bennett proudly displays one of his GRAMMYs at the 37th Annual GRAMMY Awards at the Shrine Auditorium in Los Angeles, March 1, 1995.

"I'VE FOUND I HAVE AN IMPULSE THAT ON OCCASION, WHEN EVERYONE ELSE IS GOING LEFT, I'LL TAKE A RIGHT! NOT TO BE STUBBORN, BUT TO GO DOWN A DIFFERENT CREATIVE PATH AND SEE WHAT I DISCOVER. YOU CAN'T REST ON YOUR SUCCESS, AND YOU NEED TO ALWAYS BE EXPLORING AND TESTING NEW CONCEPTS."

—TONY BENNETT

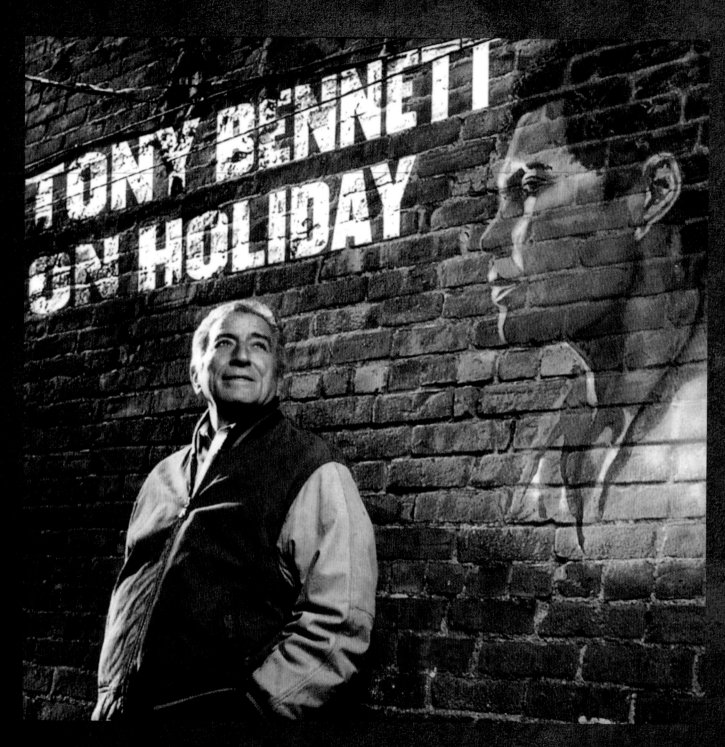

Tony poses in front of a mural of Billie Holiday's profile (based on his painting of her) on the cover of
Tony Bennett on Holiday, *released in February 1997.*

With the artistic freedom Tony had secured, it was now possible for him to pay homage to some of the artists and composers whose gifts had inspired his life. In summer 1995, he recorded the album *Here's to the Ladies*, with arrangements written by Jorge Calandrelli and Bill Holman. He honored Peggy Lee with "I'm in Love Again," Rosemary Clooney with "Tenderly," and Ella Fitzgerald with "You Showed Me the Way." Also included were songs by or made famous by Ethel Merman, Dinah Washington, and Judy Garland among others.

The album won a GRAMMY and was the theme of a star-studded December 1, 1995, CBS television special, *Tony Bennett: Here's to the Ladies, A Concert of Hope*, a fundraiser for the Center on Addiction and Substance Abuse at Columbia University. The studio audience at the Dorothy Chandler Theatre in Hollywood was also packed with celebrities, including Bob and Delores Hope. During the program, former first lady Betty Ford and President Bill Clinton were honored for their contributions to the fight against drugs. The evening ended with the cast assembled onstage—along with President Clinton, former president Ford, and Betty Ford—with Tony as he sang a moving rendition of Kurt Weill's song, "Lost in the Stars."

Billie Holiday, one of the singers represented on *Here's to the Ladies*, received a full tribute in 1997 with *Tony Bennett on Holiday*, which won the 1998 GRAMMY for Best Traditional Pop Vocal Album. One track that marries the technology of the time and uses it to create a unique duet is a Billie Holiday/Count Basie performance of Billie's "God Bless the Child" with Tony's voice electronically added in a historical recording produced by Phil Ramone.

* * *

"I GOT IN TOUCH WITH ONE OF [BILLIE HOLIDAY'S] FORMER ACCOMPANISTS, BOBBY PRATT, AND WE TALKED ABOUT SONGS SHE SANG. I WANTED TO INCLUDE SOME BALLADS ASSOCIATED WITH HER, BUT ALSO SOME OF THOSE THINGS SHE DID EARLY ON—'WHAT A LITTLE MOONLIGHT CAN DO,' WITH TEDDY WILSON, LESTER YOUNG, AND BENNY GOODMAN, AND HER RECORD OF 'LAUGHING AT LIFE' HAVE ALWAYS BEEN AMONG MY FAVORITES."

—TONY BENNETT

By the late 1990s, hundreds of stories had been written and television features produced that focused on how "cool" Tony Bennett had become with young audiences. Reflecting on that time period, Tony recently told me,

> What I noticed when performing at that time was that there was an increasing number of younger people attending our concerts, and if being "cool" meant that the songs we sang were being heard by a group of listeners who didn't have to worry about peer pressure if they listened to standards, then our goals were being achieved. Music is not something that should be sold as a commodity. Music is a gift, and we should be allowed to hear as many different kinds of musical expressions as we can and then make personal judgments on what we like best.

Tony tapped into this zeitgeist as the inspiration for his next album, 1998's *The Playground*. Tony and the Ralph Sharon Quartet (the wonderful guitarist Gray Sargent had been added to the trio) went into the Hit Factory in New York in June to record a concept album that would contain songs that would appeal to everyone—even the youngest members of the audience. "What we wanted to do, through the songs, was to let young children know that they should always try to 'Ac-Cent-Tchu-Ate the Positive' or to try to 'Put on a Happy Face'; to be positive 'When You Wish Upon a Star.' And then there were songs written just for kids like Joe Raposo's 'Bein' Green,' and 'Little Things.' I sang 'Bein' Green,' with Kermit the Frog when he was a guest on the *Live by Request* TV special. Joe Raposo had such a great gift for writing for young people, and songs can give people of any age hope!"

One of Tony's favorite songs on the CD, and one that had great personal significance to him, was a Walter Donaldson song from the 1930s, "My Mom." Tony's father taught the song to Tony and his brother John and asked them to sing it to their mother when she came home after a long day's work as a seamstress. The performance on *The Playground* is deeply felt and moving. In the 1973 Duke Ellington autobiography *Music Is My Mistress*, he writes a chapter on Tony Bennett. Duke mentions what a positive and loving family Tony had, how much he enjoyed knowing them, and what "wonderful optimists" they were. When he mentions Tony's mother, he refers to her as "Tony's beautiful mother" (see page 36). Now came a time in Tony's recording career when he could create a musical expression of love and admiration for his friend.

In May 1999, the year the world commemorated the centennial of Duke's birth, Tony recorded *Bennett Sings Ellington: Hot and Cool* at the Hit Factory. Like all Bennett recordings in this era—a time when he had total control over content and all aspects of the finished project—the results were singularly wonderful and timeless. Along with Ralph Sharon's Quartet, Tony invited two jazz legends, trumpeter Wynton Marsalis and trombonist Al Grey, as guests on several of the tracks. Additionally, to replicate the Ellington violinist Ray Nance role on a couple of selections, Tony added the gifted Joel Smirnoff. The orchestra was conducted by Jorge Calandrelli, and Ralph Burns was commissioned to write the big band charts. Among the fourteen selections of Ellington classics they recorded was a song whose title I always thought best described what I've learned over decades of conversations with Tony Bennett—"I'm Just a Lucky So and So." The song was included in his June 1962 Carnegie Hall concert, where, at thirty-five, he sang it with such a deep connection to the lyrics. Now, after living another thirty-seven years, you hear how his joy has only deepened on the 2000 GRAMMY Award–winning album. As Ellington had observed years earlier (see page 37), "He's a big beautiful man. With all of his greatness, his hat size never needed to be larger than his artistic stature."

Tony recorded Bennett Sings Ellington: Hot and Cool *to celebrate the centennial of Duke Ellington's birth in 1999.*

Duke, *Tony Bennett's striking mixed-media portrait of Duke Ellington from 1979.*

6

an AMERICAN CLASSIC: *the* TWENTY-FIRST CENTURY

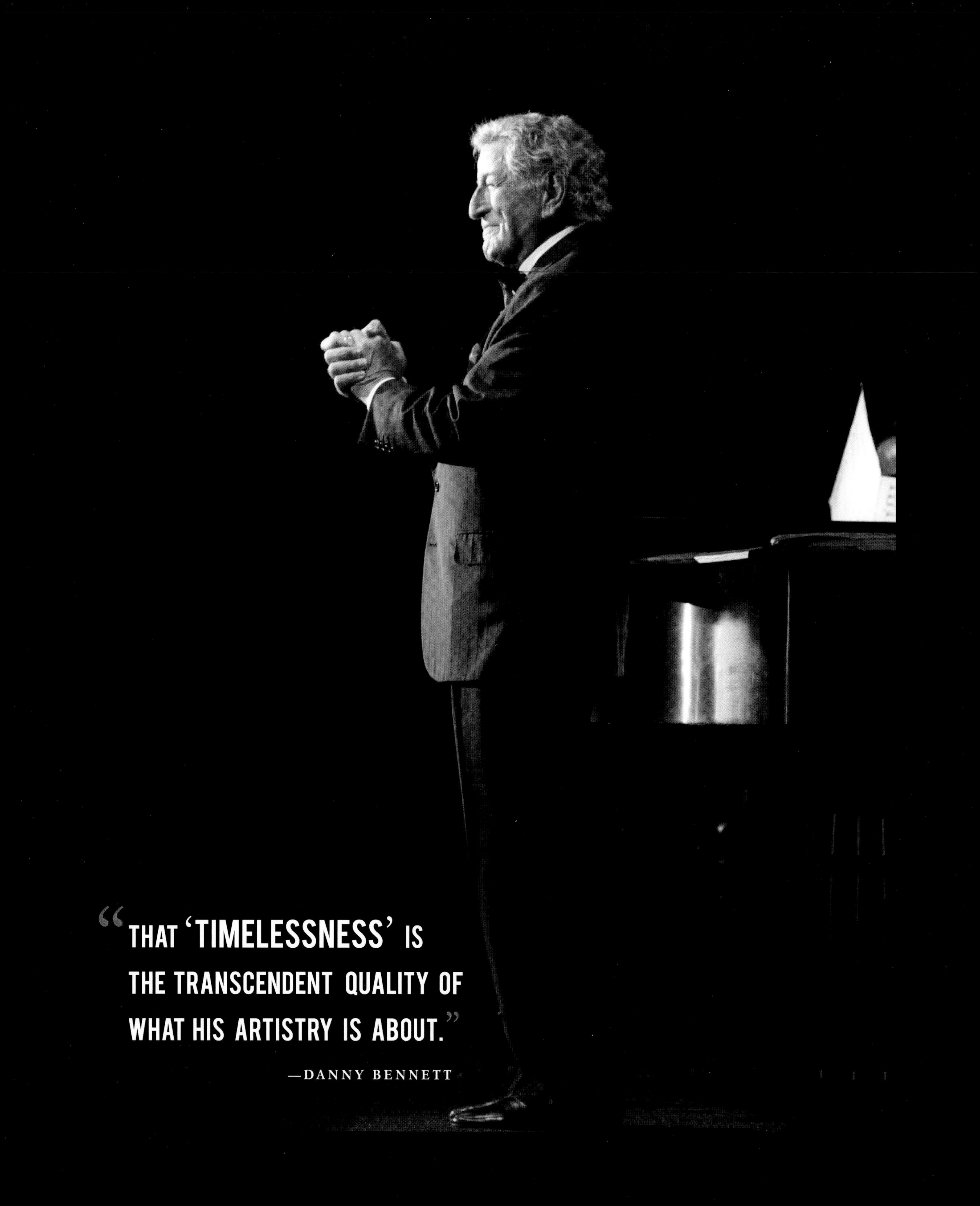

"THAT 'TIMELESSNESS' IS
THE TRANSCENDENT QUALITY OF
WHAT HIS ARTISTRY IS ABOUT."

—DANNY BENNETT

In spring 2001, several months after Tony received a GRAMMY Lifetime Achievement Award, he invited some of the most talented artists in popular music to join him for a series of recorded duets. The result was *Playing with My Friends: Bennett Sings the Blues*, released in November 2001. The CD is imbued with Count Basie's spirit and the blues he discovered in Kansas City in the 1930s: Tony and Stevie Wonder perform the Basie/Joe Williams classic "Every Day I Have the Blues," and Ray Charles and Tony duet on the Jimmy Rushing/Basie tune "Evenin'." Tony solos on the Joe Turner composition "Old Piney Brown Is Gone," but for this album it becomes "Old Count Basie Is Gone." B. B. King and Tony set the tone for the sessions with "Let the Good Times Roll," and that's just what happened during the recordings with, among other guests, Natalie Cole, Billy Joel, Bonnie Raitt, and Diana Krall.

"WHAT A WONDERFUL WORLD"

At the start of the new century it was time for Tony to conduct a musical master's class on perhaps the artist he most reveres in music, Louis Armstrong.

In addition to Tony's appreciation of Louis as a jazz master, he also had a friendship with him that was deepened when he and their mutual friend Bobby Hackett would go to Armstrong's New York home in Queens, and the three of them would listen to music that Louis chose from his extensive record library. "What great memories," Tony told me, "and Louis so appreciated Bobby's gift as a player, the beautiful sound he created on cornet." In 1970, Tony presented Louis with a portrait he had painted of Armstrong. "I gave it to him after a command performance we did, and he really liked it. He said, 'Tony you've out-Rembrandted Rembrandt!'"

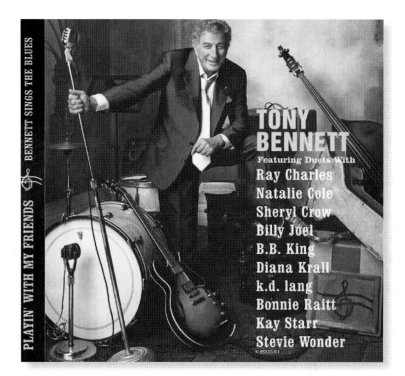

PREVIOUS PAGES: *Tony Bennett onstage at the first annual Exploring the Arts Gala at Rockefeller Center in New York, September, 2007.* OPPOSITE: *Tony at the Sons of Italy Foundation twentieth anniversary gala at the National Building Museum, Washington, DC, May 22, 2008.* ABOVE: *Album cover for the Count Basie–inspired* Playing with My Friends: Bennett Sings the Blues, *released in November 2001.*

One of the musical highlights of the *MTV Unplugged* album was a duet featuring k.d. lang and Tony singing "Moonglow"; she and Tony also performed "Keep the Faith, Baby" together on *Playing with My Friends*. The professional and personal chemistry between them was so strong that Tony invited k.d. to partner with him on a Louis Armstrong tribute album. *A Wonderful World* was recorded in March 2002 in Englewood and released the same year in November. An insight into their feelings for each other is evident in an ABC News interview after the album's release, in which Tony commented on Lang's singing: "Next to Judy Garland, she's the best singer I've ever heard. . . . When she sings, I can actually see angels. That's how good she sings." In a way similar to many of Bennett's other younger musical collaborators, k.d. responded: "I see something in him that he can teach me and, you know, entrust in me all the knowledge and wisdom that he's had over the years. And he's graciously, generously handing it to me."

The March 2002 sessions for the Armstrong tribute also brought Dae Bennett directly into one of Tony's album projects. "I'd been enjoying enough success at our Hillside Studio in Englewood," he told me, "that we had to create a larger recording facility, and that's how the big, 6,500-foot, multiroom Bennett Studios in Englewood came about. The space had formally been the Englewood train station." Dae had installed a 500-foot underground cable from the studio to the 1,200-seat John Harms Theatre so he could offer clients the opportunity to record in a space that replicated an onstage performance, and this is where the *A Wonderful World* sessions were held.

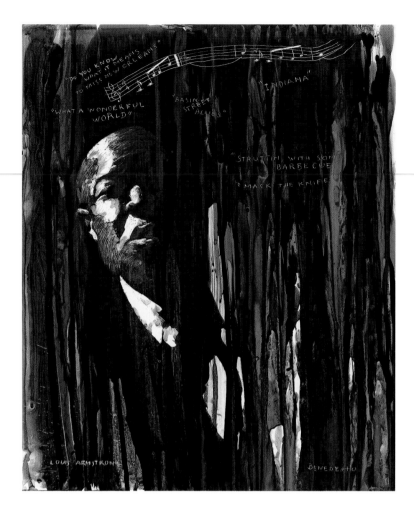

Louis Armstrong *by Tony Bennett, scratchboard and gouache.*

"**THE BOTTOM LINE OF ANY COUNTRY IN THE WORLD IS 'WHAT DID WE CONTRIBUTE TO THE WORLD?' WE CONTRIBUTED LOUIS ARMSTRONG.**"

—TONY BENNETT QUOTE ON
THE LOUIS ARMSTRONG HOUSE
MUSEUM HOME PAGE

Portrait of k.d. lang and Tony Bennett for the A Wonderful World *album cover.*

The album was produced by T Bone Burnett and featured Lee Musiker on piano (he had replaced Ralph Sharon, who earlier in the year decided that he wanted to spend more time with his family) and the rest of Tony's quartet—Gray Sargent on guitar, Paul Langosch on bass, and Clayton Cameron on drums. At the 2004 GRAMMYs, *A Wonderful World* won in the Best Traditional Pop Vocal Album category (for Dae that was one of four GRAMMY Award–winning albums that year that he recorded at Bennett Studio)—the perfect way to remind a twenty-first century audience of the importance of Louis Armstrong's legacy to the world.

In 2004, Tony assembled another outstanding creative team at the Bennett Studio's John Harms Theatre to record *The Art of Romance* album. The orchestra was conducted by Academy Award–winning composer/arranger Johnny Mandel. The producer was the legendary Phil Ramone,

who had worked with Sinatra, Bob Dylan, and Paul McCartney, among others. In addition to the album's classic repertoire (including songs by writers like Johnny Mercer, Jerome Kern, and Harold Arlen), Ramone included music by the next generation of song craftspeople such as Stephen Sondheim, David Frishberg, Mandel, and Alan and Marilyn Bergman).

Tony's superb singing was highlighted by great arrangements (Johnny Mandel, Jorge Calandrelli, and Lee Musiker), and guest soloists Phil Woods on saxophone and Candido Camero on drums. Along with his ever-present sketchbook that Tony carries with him to capture on paper an inspiring face or scene, he also carries a notebook to write down random thoughts he has about possible song lyrics. The *Art of Romance* album allowed him to publicly share one such concept. To the music of Django Reinhardt's 1940 tune "Nuages" (the original version has French lyrics by Jacques Larue), Tony's words were added, and the result was "All For You":

> When you turned around and looked into my eyes
> It was just the moment when I realized
> That my life had just begun
> And my past faded away
> All I do is hope and pray
> That our love will always stay
>
> Now my world is so alive
> My dreams came true
> You're the spirit that I need
> It's all from you
>
> Every moment that I live my whole life through
> Now I'll look into your eyes and live for you . . .

The last page of a letter written by Louis Armstrong to Tony Bennett in 1966.

Also in 2004, Columbia Records released the five-CD, 110-track collection, *Fifty Years: The Artistry of Tony Bennett*, a sequel to the *Forty Years* collection. Danny and Dae Bennett once again were executive producer and mixing engineer, respectively, and the compilation producers were Didier C. Deutsch and Mark G. Wilder. Hours, days, and months were spent by the team listening to and evaluating each recording. "There was just so much material," Dae told me,

Phil Ramone, *ink on paper portrait by Tony Bennett.*

and everything had to be listened to with critical ears. Tony had to hear each track and approve it, and Danny and I were so grateful for Didier Deutsch's skills. He was like a walking encyclopedia who knew of any cover recording that might be in the Columbia archives. We shared another sensibility about the project, and that was that so often when people do these remastering projects they're tempted to try to make it something better than it was somehow. And somehow I always felt that was like colorizing *Citizen Kane.* I like just preserving something and just bringing it into these new formats so it can live on in history forever. With Didier, we would always have a stack of vinyl so if we came across something we weren't sure of, we could actually go back and listen to the vinyl.

Those 30th Street Studio recordings came to us in three tracks. . . . The original stereo and the third track was orchestral left and right, and then in the middle was Tony's voice, with any reverb married together on one track. When you listen to tracks individually, you're like, "Oh, my God, what are we going do?" But then you split the orchestra, put Tony up the middle, and just fix the bounce and it's like, "Oh, there it is." And all of a sudden the sound pops, and you can go, "Wow. That's that 30th Street Studio sound." It's just so amazing, and it's just three tracks!

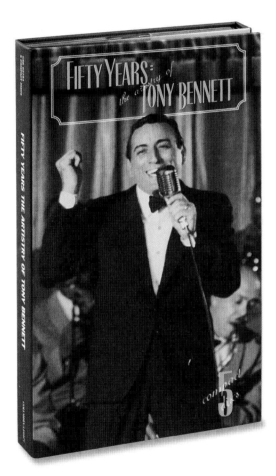

Cover to Columbia's landmark 2004 box set Fifty Years: The Artistry of Tony Bennett, *which contained an astounding 110 tracks over five CDs.*

After decades of listening and recording many artists and genres of music, Dae reflected on his father's artistry: "The great lesson about him, his career, his artistry, and what it has taught me . . . what I have learned from it, is there is a thread of quality that runs all the way through his career. It's there from the very start in the 1950s to right now, some seventy years later!"

" BY SPENDING SO MUCH TIME WITH TONY'S CATALOGUE, IT DEFINITELY GIVES YOU AN INTERESTING PERSPECTIVE ON HIS LIFE AND HOW HE LEARNED THAT QUALITY IS IMPORTANT, AND IT'S ALWAYS WORTH SPENDING THE EXTRA TIME AND EFFORT TO GET THERE. "

—DAE BENNETT

Danny has also observed in Tony the value of caring and bringing your best game to whatever you're doing. "I remember one time I was having dinner with Tony," he said, "and we were just talking about phrasing. I asked him something about phrasing when he sings, and then, I swear, for forty-five minutes, he was talking about how he articulates the word 'love,' and whether he emphasizes the *L* or he can hang on the *V*. . . . I was stunned. I've never heard him talk that way. The next day I was thinking about it, and said to him, 'You should do a book about music, like what you told me last night,' and he laughed, 'What are you talking about?' But it reveals just how much he cares about everything he does."

When Tony received an honorary Doctor of Music degree from George Washington University in May 2001, he had the attention of thousands of graduates (many who recently had become fans) and their families (many who had been fans for decades). At the ceremony, held on the National Mall, he urged the students not to abandon their ideals and the values they'd developed up to this point in their lives.

I grew up in an America that prized quality in so many aspects of our national life, and because of that, we became an international standard by which all others were judged. In music, we had a generation of composers who wrote songs that will last forever. Perhaps the single biggest musical contribution we made to world culture is jazz. This music represents who we are as a people because the foundation of jazz is freedom of expression, just as our Declaration of Independence guarantees the American people."

Danny Bennett, who is now president of the record label that was first established by Norman Granz to capture and preserve the artistry of Ella Fitzgerald and subsequently recorded some of the most important jazz albums, recently told me, "I just read a quote attributed to Count Basie. He said that jazz is for the young at heart and that the young at heart will always love jazz, which is great. But see, what he's saying is that it transcends. And what's interesting is what we're doing here at Verve is we're finding this is so true. There is this new movement where jazz is becoming the foundation for all these kids as an alternative to other music. I'm really proud of being able to be the gatekeeper, not only of the crown jewel of the music that you and I know very well belongs in a museum, but a museum of the people, and be able to get that message across. If I could just do one ounce of what I've done for Tony for the rest of the Verve catalogue that I'm in charge of right now, then I can put my head on the pillow."

" AN AMERICAN CLASSIC "

As Tony celebrated his eightieth birthday on August 3, 2006, he was still at the top of his game as a performing artist. His favorite place to be has always been on a stage inspiring audiences, and in turn the inspiration he receives from the public feeds his creativity when he returns to the recording studio. Tony Bennett has been singing "duets" since he and Rosemary Clooney costarred in 1950 on *Songs for Sale* (see page 69). In any number of live concerts in his career, he has sung with Frank Sinatra, Ella Fitzgerald, Judy Garland, Lena Horne, and other artists from the golden age of American popular song. When the concept for the 2006 *Duets: An American Classic* was being developed, Tony told me that he was eager to work with artists such as Bono, Paul McCartney, Stevie Wonder, Barbra Streisand, Elton John, Sting, Billy Joel, Celine Dion, Michael Bublé, and others.

"I've always been grateful for the wisdom and knowledge that was passed on to me from mentors like Duke Ellington, Sinatra, and Count Basie. For me, just being around them and observing how they worked was such a valuable education, and if I can pass off some of the history and what I've learned in music after over almost seventy years of performing, it is such a personal reward."

Tony Bennett
Duets
An American Classic

Featuring
Bono
Michael Bublé
Elvis Costello
Celine Dion
Dixie Chicks
Billy Joel
Elton John
Juanes
Diana Krall
k.d. lang
John Legend
Paul McCartney
Tim McGraw
George Michael
Sting
Barbra Streisand
James Taylor
Stevie Wonder

The 2006 Duets: An American Classic *album cover, which featured a collage of Tony's face made up of over a thousand circular portraits of him.*

FROM LEFT TO RIGHT: *Danny Bennett, Phil Ramone, Dae Bennett, and Tony Bennett pose at Bennett Studios in Englewood, New Jersey, while working on the groundbreaking, award-winning album* Duets: An American Classic, *March 2006.*

Danny Bennett told me, "I see these performances less as duets and more as collaborations." Although the guest artists represented a broad spectrum of popular music, the songs chosen for the CD were all standards Tony originally introduced to the world: for example "Just in Time" with Michael Bublé (a 1956 Tony Bennett hit), "The Best Is Yet to Come" with Diana Krall (introduced by Tony in 1959), and Elton John joining Tony on his 1953 hit, "Rags to Riches." Not only did the songs reflect Tony's commitment to great music, but as Danny pointed out, his collaborators learned something about Tony Bennett's recording techniques:

It's very important to note that with all the new technology, Tony chose to record the same way he has since 1950, and that is to go into the studio and do a live recording. The most impressive aspect of this project—especially for the younger artists—was to come into the studio and not overdub or employ all kinds of editing tricks, but to stand next to Tony and record live. They discovered Tony doesn't even use earphones—that he tries to keep the sessions as live and spontaneous as possible. Many of the artists left their session saying this was the way they wanted to record in the future.

" BELIEVING IN THE POWER OF ART TO ENNOBLE ORDINARY LIVES, [TONY BENNETT] SINGS WHAT HE FEELS WITH A RARE MIXTURE OF HUMILITY AND PRIDE....GRATITUDE AND JOY, GRUFFNESS AND BEAUTY BALANCE EACH OTHER PERFECTLY IN SINGING THAT HAS GROWN MORE RHYTHMICALLY ACUTE WITH EACH PASSING YEAR. "

—STEPHEN HOLDEN, *NEW YORK TIMES*, AUGUST 2, 2006

From February to June 2006, in between dozens of live concerts, Tony and his singing partners recorded in a variety of facilities, including Capitol Records in Hollywood, Abbey Road Studios in London, and Bennett Studios in Englewood. Joining Tony, Danny, and Dae in

producing the sessions was the award-winning producer Phil Ramone.

When the sessions were complete, Tony called me to say what a memorable project it had been. "We had such a great spirit at each session, and it was like recording with old friends." Danny told me, "It's important to understand the interaction and spontaneity when Tony records with younger artists. There is such a mutual respect; Tony treats each artist as an equal—it's musician to musician. Some of the comments the guest artists made to me and Dae consistently were focused on how thrilling it was to watch Tony continually reinvent himself and how he created the environment for the honest performances you hear on the CD. Each session was like a master's class for the guest performers, and that's what makes the project extremely special."

Released in September 2006, *Duets: An American Classic* reached No. 3 on the *Billboard* 200 and went on to become one of the best-selling CDs of the year. It won three GRAMMYs, including one for Best Pop Collaboration with Vocal for the Tony Bennett/Stevie Wonder

duet "For Once in My Life." It also became the inspiration for another Bennett TV special, *Tony Bennett: An American Classic*, directed by Rob Marshall. The November 2006 special won seven Emmys (Danny received one as producer and Dae one for sound mixing), including the coveted award for Outstanding Variety, Music or Comedy Special.

Also in 2006, Tony made a memorable appearance on the November 11 episode of *Saturday Night Live*, appearing as "Anthony Dominick Benedetto" in a sketch with host and Alec Baldwin (impersonating Tony), on Baldwin's recurring *SNL* talk show parody skit *The Tony Bennett Show*.

ABOVE FROM LEFT TO RIGHT: *Tony and Danny pose with their GRAMMYs for* Duets: An American Classic *and "For Once in My Life" at the 49th Annual GRAMMY Awards, Los Angeles, February 11, 2007; Michael Bublé and Tony Bennett in a still from the Emmy Award–winning TV special* Tony Bennett: An American Classic, *filmed at the Los Angeles Theatre; a still from Tony's 2006 appearance with Alec Baldwin on* Saturday Night Live, *during Baldwin's* The Tony Bennett Show *sketch.*

The worldwide success of *Duets* inspired a sequel project in spring 2011. As Tony performed concerts in Canada, the United States, England, and Denmark that year, he also visited recording studios in Los Angeles, Nashville, New York, London, the Bennett Studios in Englewood, and even a small Italian village in Tuscany, to collaborate with another group of gifted singers representing various generations. From Lady Gaga to Willie Nelson to Aretha Franklin and Josh Groban, some of the best and brightest talents joined Tony on this project. The same award-winning production team again captured the magic, and when I spoke to Tony that spring, he was so enthused about the sequel record:

What I've discovered in collaborating with the very talented young contemporary artists on *Duets II* is that they love to sing the American standards. . . . I've so enjoyed experiencing with them their growth as performers as we collaborated on these sessions, and if you listen to their performances on this CD, you'll discover that this new generation of artists can sing these songs as well as anyone in the past. If they can continue the journey and discover and record more of this material these great songs will never go away. I've been traveling and performing all over the world for over half a century, and these songs continue to be among America's greatest musical ambassadors, representing American quality and excellence.

When the sessions had wrapped up that summer, I had a phone conversation with producer Phil Ramone, who had just listened to the final mix of the Tony Bennett/Norah Jones recording of Kurt Weill's "Speak Low."

This was such a magical session. Tony's knowledge of the history of the American song just fascinates me. Not only is he the great interpreter of this material, but he knows the history of Kurt Weill and the history of the

songs he sings. Tony is also, I think, the greatest interpreter of the genius of the Gershwins. It was wonderful watching Sheryl Crow and Tony perform together on the classic "The Man I Love" [also known as "The Girl I Love," as on the CD]. Tony loved the arrangement, noting "Jorge Calandrelli wrote a beautiful orchestration for the session. I thing Jorge really captured the magnificence of George Gershwin's ability as a composer. The orchestration is classical . . . and then Sheryl and I did something that hadn't been done with the song, and that was to alter some of the lyrics, so we could sing it together. I think it worked beautifully.

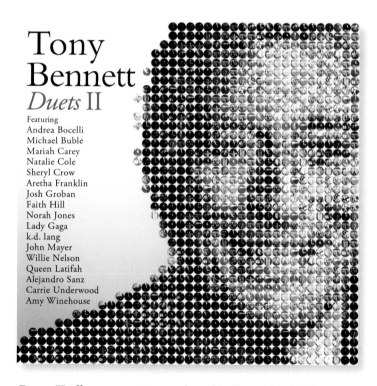

Duets II *album cover; it was released in September 2011.*

"I TOLD HIM TO CHANGE HIS NAME TO TONY BENNETT. BUT YOU KNOW SOMETHING? WITH HIS TALENT, HE'D BE JUST AS POPULAR WITH HIS REAL NAME, ANTONIO BENEDETTO."
—BOB HOPE

One additional production component added to the recording session for *Duets II* was the decision to film every session with a crew led by Academy Award–winning cinematographer Dion Beebe. "We're doing a major documentary called *The Zen of Bennett*," Danny told me as the album was being recorded. "It will be focused on the philosophical journey of Tony's career. That 'timelessness' is the transcendent quality of what his artistry is about. . . . It's like looking at a great painting—the past fades away, and you suspend thinking about the future; you feel so alive in that moment you're experiencing. Artistically, for me, that defines the essence of Tony Bennett's success as a musical artist."

LEFT: *Tony and Phil Ramone at Capitol Studios in Hollywood during the recording of* Duets II *in February 2011. Ramone was the coproducer of that album, as well as the producer of seven other albums with Tony, including the first* Duets *(2006) and* Playing with My Friends *(2001).*

This still from the 2012 documentary The Zen of Bennett *captures John Mayer and Tony Bennett in 2011, during the recording of the Harold Arlen/Johnny Mercer classic "One for My Baby (and One More for the Road)" for* Duets II.

Tony found the presence of the cameras not an impediment, but rather an element that added to the creativity of the project. "You know how I always find singing with k.d. lang so special—she sings so beautifully and so meaningfully, she is so genuine. The film and production crew constructed a different set for each session on the album, and for my duet with k.d. on 'Blue Velvet' in Los Angeles, they created the most beautiful wall of blue velvet as a backdrop. It was so inspirational and helped k.d. and me get into just the right mood of that song."

Another thrilling moment in this historic project was when Tony and the group were invited to Andrea Bocelli's home in Tuscany to record Tony Bennett's 1953 classic, "Stranger in Paradise."

"What a wonderful experience this session was. First, we flew to Andrea's home near Pisa, Italy. Andrea invited me, Susan, and our team to his beautiful house—which has a recording studio—right near the ocean. I loved singing with him, and as soon as the session was over, he treated us to a wonderful home-cooked Italian meal. It was an unforgettable day."

Speaking on the results of the session, Phil Ramone said, "When you listen to this beautiful recording, you realize this is not a competition of two bel canto–trained tenors; you feel their mutual admiration and respect in this tender and beautiful record."

That session also gave Tony an opportunity to connect with his Italian roots, which has been the foundation of his creative spirit. The film crew captured Tony singing "'O Sole Mio" on a mountaintop in the home village of his father, in Calabria. "When I was growing up, the first singing voice I heard that made me want to sing was my father Giovanni Benedetto's singing voice. I loved his singing, and my relatives would always tell stories about my how my dad, when he was a young man, would stand atop the mountains in Podargoni and sing, and everyone in the valley would stop what they were doing just so they could hear him."

During his trip to Italy in March 2011 to record "Stanger in Paradise" with Andrea Bocelli for Duets II*, Tony visited the his father's hometown of Podargoni, in the Calabria region—and made time to sing "'O Sole Mio" across a valley there.*

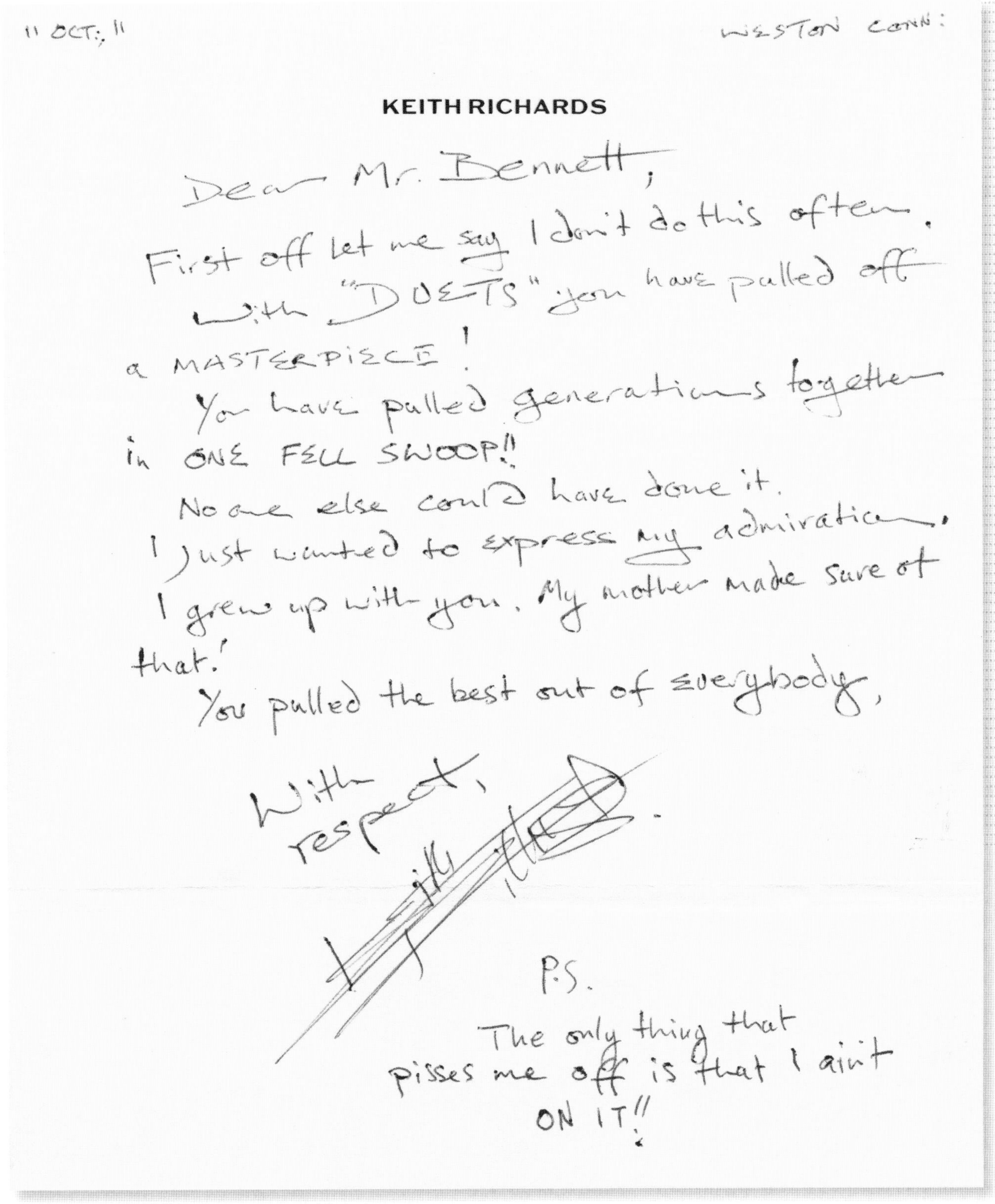

KEITH RICHARDS

Dear Mr. Bennett,

First off let me say I don't do this often.
With "DUETS" you have pulled off
a MASTERPIECE!

You have pulled generations together
in ONE FELL SWOOP!!

No one else could have done it.
I just wanted to express my admiration.
I grew up with you. My mother made sure of
that!

You pulled the best out of everybody,

With
respect,

[signature]

P.S.
The only thing that
pisses me off is that I aint
ON IT!!

*A letter written on October 11, 2011, by the Rolling Stones' Keith Richards
to Tony Bennett, congratulating him on* Duets II.

Carrie Underwood and Tony Bennett in 2011, recording "It Had to Be You" for Duets II.

Tony looks out the window during one of his trips in March 2011 to record for Duets II. The album was recorded in studios across the United States, and in London and Italy.

Because the sessions were being documented on film, we can still experience one of the most poignant parts of the making of *Duets II*. The Tony Bennett/Amy Winehouse collaboration took place at the Abbey Road Studios in London, in March 2011. Before the session, Tony had been very much looking forward to recording with her because he appreciated her jazz instincts (her parents loved the music, and she had grown up listening to her parents' records). He later reflected,

Contemporary popular music artists, for the most part, have experienced mostly rock music in their lives. But along comes Amy Winehouse, who has such an innate sense and feeling for singing jazz. Amy's idol in music is the late Dinah Washington, truly one of the best singers I've known in my life. . . . I found Amy to be one of the most focused and professional artists I collaborated with on this project. She is gifted to be able to be such

a spontaneous singer—to be in the moment. You sense that feeling in every note she sings on "Body and Soul." I was just knocked out by her performance, and so was everyone else at the session.

In the video of the session, you can empathize with Amy as she nervously questions her ability: "I don't want to waste your time," she says to Tony, who responds, "You're not wasting my time. We have all day, and we'll stay until we get what we want!" His quiet mentoring and counsel began to dissipate all of her self-doubt, and they created a recording of "Body and Soul" that would go on to win the 2012 GRAMMY for Best Pop Duo/Group Performance. It was the last record Amy Winehouse recorded before her death, four months after the session.

Phil Ramone summed up Tony's empathy for Amy and for all the talented singers he worked on both *Duets* albums: "The entire list of guest artists we produced so much appreciated Tony Bennett's warmth and artistic generosity. For many it was one of the career highlights they'll always remember—I know I will!" As for what Tony tried to communicate to a new generation of performers, he told me, "Fame can be very threatening. You might work hard and become very famous and then go right down and be broke. . . . I tried to get them to think about how, if you want longevity in show business, you shouldn't be obsessed with thinking only of fame, you should think of quality, and then you stay in the business all the time." *Duets II* won the GRAMMY for Best Traditional Pop Vocal Album in 2012.

Also in 2012, Tony went back into studios in New York; Nashville; Englewood; Davie, Florida; and Guadalajara, Mexico to record the *Viva Duets* CD, which featured some of the top Latin American singers, including Christina Aguilera, Gloria Estefan, and Marc Anthony. After its release in October 2012, it became a major hit throughout the Americas.

After finishing *Duets II*, Tony began preparing for a summer tour of Europe that would include sold-out concerts in seven countries. On this tour he was joined by his daughter Antonia, who had blossomed into a wonderful jazz singer. Just before the tour started, I spoke with Danny, who still was processing something his dad had recently said to him.

I called Tony to wish him a happy Father's Day last week. We began talking and reflecting on the upcoming year and his eighty-fifth birthday on August 3. He said to me, "Listen, I've got to tell you what my premise is—I want to prove that when I get older, that if I continue to be blessed by good health, that I'm going to strive to get better and better." I said, "But dad, you're eighty-five-years old!" and he replied, "But that's beside the point." To which I said, "But that is the point." "No, no," he responded, "When I'm 102, I want to be singing *better* than I am now." And there you have the secret of Tony Bennett's spirit . . . the essence of who he's always been. Here is someone at eighty-five telling you "that's beside the point!"

Tony Bennett and his daughter Antonia Bennett perform together at the Robert S. Whitney Hall in Louisville, Kentucky, April 1, 2011.

"TONY'S CONSTANT CREATIVITY ONSTAGE, EVERY NIGHT, ALWAYS AMAZES ME. ENDLESS MELODIC VARIATIONS, BUT ALWAYS WITH THE MELODY OF THE SONG AT THE HEART OF IT. HIS INCREDIBLE VOCAL TECHNIQUE IS ALWAYS IN SERVICE TO THE MUSIC, CONVEYING THE BEAUTY AND MEANING OF THE SONG. HE HAS ALWAYS BEEN AND CONTINUES TO BE AN INSPIRATION TO ME, EACH AND EVERY NIGHT, FOR THE TWENTY-PLUS YEARS I'VE HAD THE GREAT FORTUNE TO WORK AND PLAY WITH HIM."

—GRAY SARGENT, GUITARIST WITH THE
TONY BENNETT QUARTET

For Duets II, Lady Gaga did a duet with Tony of the Rodgers and Hart show tune "The Lady Is a Tramp"; she signed her sheet music from the session for Tony, including a small drawing of the two of them, shown here.

In late May 2011, Tony Bennett appeared on the finale of *American Idol*. This would be yet another triumph for him and Danny in their ongoing strategy to break through demographic and generational barriers. Danny and I had a conversation about Tony's *American Idol* appearance, where he and finalist Haley Reinhart sang Irving Berlin's "Steppin' Out with My Baby."

"Here's an eighty-five-year-old icon performing with a talented twenty-one-year-old woman, and they're singing a song that at the time was over sixty years old. They were seen by a national audience of 29 million people. He came out onstage and brought great music to a massive young audience, and he was met with overwhelming gratitude and acceptance. And that's the thing about great art—it transcends. Young audiences recognize Tony Bennett's greatness as a performer and as a person."

Another guest on that evening's program was Lady Gaga, and Danny got a chance to speak with her. "Tony and I were chatting with her after the *Idol* show, and I thanked her for taking time out of her very intense schedule to collaborate with Tony on the *Duets II* CD on 'The Lady Is a Tramp.' She said, as she put her arms around Tony, 'Thank me? Thank him . . . I'd be nothing without Tony Bennett.'" That evening turned out to be the foundation of a collaboration that was unprecedented in popular music. Over the next several months, Tony and Lady Gaga's teams organized recording sessions that began in the summer of 2013 with Danny and Dae joining their dad in the project. In phone conversations at that time, Tony told me how excited he was about the set list he and Lady Gaga had agreed upon. "Among the songs we've chosen, we have Cole Porter, Jerome Kern, and Billy Strayhorn—plus two songs by Irving Berlin [including the title track] and two songs written by Duke Ellington. I've also asked Paul Horn to join us on flute [he'd been a guest on Tony's 1966 tele-vision special, *Singer Presents Tony Bennett*; see page 57] for our version of Nat Cole's 'Nature Boy.'"

In a September 2014 interview with the *London Telegraph*, Lady Gaga, who had won a jazz vocal competition when she was fifteen years old, revealed her affection and appreciation of the music Tony Bennett has been bringing to life for decades: "This is the Great American Songbook. It's meant to be sung till the end of time. And 'Cheek to Cheek' is the most simple and most beautiful way you can describe this relationship. Nothing matters except that we are together and we are having a conversation with jazz." Jorge Calandrelli and Marion Evans were commissioned to write the arrangements, and Tony's group included pianists Mike Renzi and Tom Lanier, Gray Sargent on guitar, drummer Harold Jones, and Marshall Wood on bass. Lady Gaga invited talented trumpeter Brian Newman and his jazz quintet to participate as well.

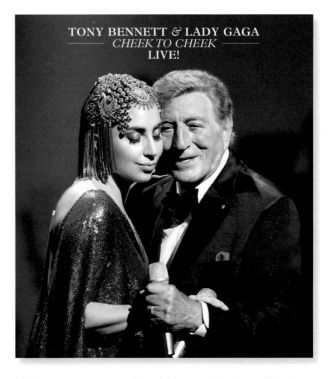

The Tony Bennett and Lady Gaga: Cheek to Cheek Live! *concert was recorded at the Rose Theater at Lincoln Center in New York on July 28, 2014, and aired on PBS on October 24, 2014. The DVD and Blu-Ray (cover shown here) of the show were released in September 2014.*

The completed CD, *Cheek to Cheek*, was released in September 2014. The CD climbed high on pop charts all over the world, hitting number one on the *Billboard* 200; the song "Anything Goes" topped the *Billboard*'s Jazz Digital Songs Chart. It also spawned a PBS special and a thirty-six–performance yearlong international tour.

The tour ran from late 2014 until the eve of Tony Bennett's eighty-ninth birthday, with venues that included the North Sea and Copenhagen Jazz Festivals, Royal Albert Hall in London, the Hollywood Bowl, and Radio City Music Hall. The last venue on the tour was the Kennedy Center for the Performing Arts in Washington, DC, which I had the good fortune to attend. Lady Gaga had an early birthday surprise for Tony, and the audience stood and applauded as a very large birthday cake she had ordered for the occasion was brought onstage and she led the audience in singing "Happy Birthday." Later backstage, Tony and Lady Gaga were so generous with their praise for the people who made the CD/tour possible, and the affection and appreciation they had for one another was obvious to all.

ABOVE: *Tony Bennett and Lady Gaga perform during their* Cheek to Cheek *tour at the New Orleans Jazz Festival, April 26, 2015.*

THANK YOU
VERY MUCH!

BENIRDETTO

Tony,
I ♡ you.. You really
are beyond special.
Thank you for believing
"in" me.

Love, Lady Gaga

"I AM FASCINATED BY THIS PARTNERSHIP BETWEEN LADY GAGA AND TONY BENNETT....HE HAS ALLOWED HER TO PRESENT A WHOLE DIFFERENT SIDE OF HERSELF IN A SECURE WAY THAT'S MIND-BOGGLING....HE'S FOUND YOUTH IN HER, AND SHE'S FOUND COMFORT IN HIM. IT'S MAGIC. I LOVE THAT.'

—PRESIDENT BILL CLINTON, INTERVIEW ON THE *QUEEN LATIFAH SHOW*, NOVEMBER 14, 2014

Lady Gaga, *a 2011 ink on paper drawing by* Tony Bennett, *signed by Lady Gaga.*

A ticket to the July 28, 2014, Tony Bennett and Lady Gaga: Cheek to Cheek Live! concert at Lincoln Center, New York.

jazz at lincoln center

1114871
273400

TONY BENNETT & LADY GAGA
CHEEK TO CHEEK: LIVE!

Level/Door
MEZZ 8

** NO seating after 6:45pm **
This ticket is non-transferrable.

Box/Row/Seat
1 4

Rose Theater
Monday, July 28, 2014 / 7:00 PM

Guest

9900000000003735387844

373844

07/28 7:00PM
MEZZ 8
1 4
5 373844
273400

frederick p. rose hall Broadway at 60th Street, 5th floor

Bill Charlap and Tony Bennett hold their GRAMMYs for Best Traditional Pop Vocal Album for The Silver Lining: The Songs of Jerome Kern, *at the 58th GRAMMY Awards at the Staples Center in Los Angeles, February 15, 2016.*

have performed with Tony and recorded with him on several occasions, and one thing I know is that San Francisco has to share his heart with his other love: jazz. Tony Bennett tells the story of how, when he first went to see Charlie Parker perform at Birdland, he was so overcome with the emotion from Parker's playing that it affected him on a physical level. For Tony, jazz has always been a visceral experience—it's in his blood. . . . Tony's singing lives and breathes in the moment—he creates, feels, and interprets spontaneously, always fresh, never by rote.

Early in his career, Tony had a music teacher who exhorted him to avoid paying too much attention to other singers; it was too easy to fall into the trap of imitation. However, by studying the great jazz soloists and learning all he could from them, he couldn't help but be original. So, as much as he loves the singing of Frank Sinatra, Billie Holiday, Fred Astaire, Bing Crosby, and Louis Armstrong, Tony is even more influenced by the stunning creations of the all-time jazz piano giant, Art Tatum. Tony was inspired by the way that Tatum would set up a melody, then spin amazing variations on the tune, before building up to a huge dramatic climax. Tony learned his own lessons from Tatum's playing, and it comes through when you hear him sing "Maybe This Time," or "Ol' Devil Moon" (on *Cloud 7*), and especially "How Do You Keep the Music Playing," where he takes that final note and stretches it upwards for an entire octave with a powerful emotional effect.

There is a certain energy and wavelength in jazz. You either get it or you don't—and Tony gets it. There are certain gatekeepers out there who try to tell you exactly who is a jazz singer and who is not. But Tony, like another one of his heroes, the immortal Duke Ellington, is unconcerned with categories. To me, Tony is absolutely a jazz singer. Whenever we have played together, he is always listening to the playing of the musicians around him, responding to their rhythmic and harmonic choices and initiating surprising and exiting musical ideas. He is part of the band! And then there is his way with a lyric. Tony always tells a story from a deep and interior place that reaches directly into the last soul in the back row of the fifth-tier balcony. His interpretations are both extemporaneous and definitive. He is the red carpet for the intentions of the composers and the lyricists. Call him a jazz singer or not, he doesn't care, but there's no denying that the musical and emotional impacts of the great jazz masters are ineffable parts of his musical makeup—without Armstrong, Tatum, Basie, and Holiday, Tony Bennett wouldn't sound like Tony Bennett. . . .

Perhaps the most important thing that Tony learned from Pops, Lester Young, and Tatum was the ideal of being both in the groove, rhythmically, and also in the moment, philosophically, and to sing from a place of spontaneous, intimate creation. In opera or musical theater, you're set in a predetermined place, and while the results can be magical, in jazz you have both the freedom and the responsibility to respond to the context and the circumstances around you. The music can never happen exactly the same twice, because each individual moment happens only once. In fact, the great drummer, Shelly Manne, once described jazz as a music where "we never play anything the same way once," which perfectly describes Tony. . . .

What you are getting with Tony is absolute emotional honesty—it's always the pure truth. Every

In a recent conversation with Tony Bennett, he told me that one of the essential truths in a creative life is that you must always be experimenting, "I've found I have an impulse that on occasion, when everyone else is going left, I'll take a right! Not to be stubborn but to go down a different creative path and see what I discover. You can't rest on you success and you need to always be exploring and testing new concepts." That personal philosophy led to, among other indelible moments in the recording studio, the Tony Bennett/Bill Evans voice and piano albums. And in the twenty-first century, Tony next elected to pay musical homage to perhaps the most revered composer of American classic song, Jerome David Kern. *The Silver Lining: The Songs of Jerome Kern* featured Tony and pianist Bill Charlap. Guesting on a few of the tracks is pianist Renee Rosnes, Charlap's wife, and about half of the recordings feature Peter Washington on bass and Kenny Washington on drums, members of the Bill Charlap Trio. The September 2015 release coincided with the 130th year of Kern's birth (1885) and the seventieth anniversary of his death, after which President Harry S. Truman issued a statement from the White House: "His melodies will live in our voices and warm our hearts for many years to come, for they are the kind of simple, honest songs that belong to no time or fashion."

True to this sentiment, when the GRAMMY award–winning CD was released, it became the number one *Billboard* jazz album. Nate Chinen's *New York Times* review of September 23, 2015, captures the spirit imbued on every track: "Jerome Kern turns out to be the ideal touchstone for Mr. Bennett: He was a suave melodist who married classical form with jazz inflection, and many of his tunes have long been standards. . . . He radiates pluck and purpose, a conviction that what matters is the drive to keep going. It's not a message to take lightly now, if indeed it ever was."

Not only does the CD represent Tony's life in music, but the cover booklet contains a beautiful "Benedetto" sketch of the composer; it truly was a Bennett family project with Danny producing, Dae recording and mixing, and granddaughter Kelsey providing some wonder photography for the package.

In October 1987, the centennial year of Kern's birth, President Ronald Reagan hosted a Kern birthday celebration in the East Room. The concert was taped for the *In Performance at the White House* series by PBS, and some of the comments delivered by the president that evening could very well be said to describe what I have observed about the life and times of Tony Bennett: "[Jerome] Kern was not content just to write songs. Like many men of genius, he wanted to take what he knew and raise it up, make it more significant, establish a higher standard for everyone who would follow. He had great faith in the intelligence of the American people and the power of the stage. He wanted to go beyond the old-fashioned musical revues and bring forth a vigorous new art form, a story told in music."

* * *

Bill Charlap and Tony Bennett on the album cover of The Silver Lining: The Songs of Jerome Kern, *released in September 2015. The album cover photograph also features Kenny Washington on drums and Peter Washington on bass.*

Bill Charlap at the Jazz Standard, *watercolor on paper by Tony Bennett.*

Tony Bennett and his family arrive at the Rainbow Room in New York for his ninetieth birthday celebration.

By 2016, the year of Tony's ninetieth birthday, he continued to blaze along a unique path he had created in American popular culture. And he continued to receive the loving support of his family. For Dae, the last two decades of professional collaboration in the studio have given him new insights and a deeper appreciation for what his father continues to accomplish:

When I look back on the '60s and '70s in the world of the music Tony loved, I see that it wasn't great at the time. It definitely wasn't. Quincy Jones recently talked about how in the '50s, early '60s, these wonderful performers—Tony, Nat Cole, Sinatra, Ella—they owned everything. They were on top of the world. And then within three months, they couldn't be heard on the radio. You have to think of how devastating that must have been to these artists. I've been involved in many projects for the last three decades, but I've really focused the last fifteen years or more on Tony's legacy. It's been very rewarding because it gives us the opportunity to first and foremost, accomplish and achieve some success together, as father and son.

It has been almost forty years since Tony, Dae, and Danny sat down and talked about the need to preserve the American popular song and the urgency to bring jazz-influenced music to a new generation. Danny is still as animated and enthused as he was at the start of the journey, "What most artists do in the first part of their career Tony continues doing now—things like breaking into new markets and being discovered by new age groups for the first time. Fans who were in their twenties and thirties when they first discovered Tony and are now over fifty years old, and their children have also discovered Tony. His audience includes people from ages twelve to ninety! It just defies gravity."

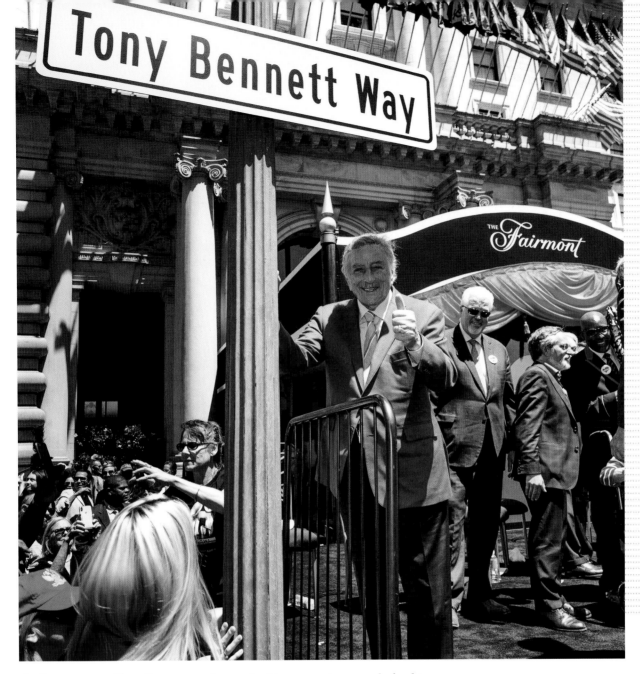

On June 2, 2018, Tony Bennett was honored with a street sign named after him on the 900 block of Mason Street in San Francisco, in front of the Fairmont Hotel, where he first performed "I Left My Heart in San Francisco" in 1961.

One of Tony's favorite quotes is "I'm still learning" (in Italian, *ancora imparo*), often attributed to an elderly Michelangelo. Danny has an up-close view of his dad and continues to be awed and inspired by what Tony learns, what he sees and hears. "He sounds better than ever and has accomplished all his many missions in life, and yet there is not a hint of complacency or settling—none. His lifelong passion for life, music, art, ideas, justice, and humanity—these are the essence of his spirit, the qualities that keep him totally engaged in each hour and day of his life. "I really feel so blessed to be able to work with him. It's kind of like someone saying, 'Hey, how would you like to work with Michelangelo?'"

* * *

> **"I AM CERTAIN THAT AFTER THE DUST OF CENTURIES HAS PASSED OVER OUR CITIES, WE, TOO, WILL BE REMEMBERED NOT FOR VICTORIES OR DEFEATS IN BATTLE OR IN POLITICS, BUT FOR OUR CONTRIBUTION TO THE HUMAN SPIRIT."**
>
> **—PRESIDENT JOHN F. KENNEDY**

A s long as humanity has the capacity to be encouraged and inspired by music, we can take collective pride in the great contribution America has made to the "human spirit" President Kennedy spoke about. Through our American standard songs like those written by the Gershwin brothers, and the music that represents our democratic ideals so eloquently—jazz, the music of "collective improvisation"—we have created some of our most important and enduring tools for cultural diplomacy. And for as long as people listen to this uniquely American body of music they will continue to celebrate the gift of one of the music's most unique and talented interpreters, Tony Bennett.

A musical notation by Tony Bennett of one of his favorite verses, from the Fred Astaire/Tommy Wolf song "Life Is Beautiful." **OPPOSITE:** *Portrait of Tony Bennett, 2016.*

APPENDIX

SPECIAL PERFORMANCES

FOR PRESIDENTS OF THE UNITED STATES
1956 Dwight D. Eisenhower

1962 John F. Kennedy

1967 Lyndon B. Johnson

1976 Gerald Ford

c. 1978 Jimmy Carter

1981, 1985 Ronald Reagan

1990 George H. W. Bush

1996, 1997, 2003 William J. Clinton

2001 George W. Bush

2013 Barack Obama

PERFORMANCE FOR BRITISH ROYALTY IN LONDON
1965 Royal Command Performance at the London Palladium in the presence of Her Majesty Queen Elizabeth II and HRH Prince Philip, Duke of Edinburgh

1966 Performance at Grosvenor House in the presence of Her Majesty the Queen Mother

1970 Performance at Buckingham Palace in the presence of HRH Prince Philip, Duke of Edinburgh

1972 National Playing Fields Association Charity Gala with Louis Armstrong in the presence of HRH Princess Alexandra

1982 Royal Variety Gala at the Barbican Theatre in the presence of TRH the Prince and Princess of Wales

1995 Royal Command Performance at the Dominion Theatre

1996 Royal Albert Hall performance in the presence of Her Majesty Queen Elizabeth II and Nelson Mandela, president of South Africa

2002 The Party at the Palace, Queen's Jubilee concert, in the presence of Her Majesty Queen Elizabeth II

2015 WellChild Benefit Performance at Royal Albert Hall with Lady Gaga in the presence of HRH Prince Henry of Wales

2016 Performance at Buckingham Palace for the Prince of Wales Foundation in the presence of HRH Prince Charles of Wales

SPECIAL AWARDS AND HONORS

1996 Primetime Emmy Awards: Outstanding Performance for a Variety or Music Program for *Tony Bennett Live by Request: A Valentine's Day Special*

1996 Cable Ace Awards: Performance in a Music Special or Series for *Tony Bennett Live by Request: A Valentine's Day Special*

1998 Juvenile Diabetes Research Foundation: Humanitarian of the Year Award

2000 United Nations: Citizen of the World Award

2000 American Cancer Society: Humanitarian Award

2000 Library of Congress Living Legend Award

2001 George Washington University: Honorary Doctor of Music Degree

2002 The King Center: Salute to Greatness Award

2002 ASCAP: Pied Piper Lifetime Achievement Award

2003 Songwriters Hall of Fame: Towering Song Award and Towering Performance Award

2005 Kennedy Center for the Performing Arts Honoree

2006 National Endowment for the Arts: Jazz Master

2006 ASCAP: Legacy Award

2006 Billboard Century Award

2007 United Nations Humanitarian Award

2007 Inductee in Civil Rights Walk of Fame

2007 Primetime Emmy Award for Individual Performance for a Variety or Music Program for *Tony Bennett: An American Classic*

2016 The Empire State Building in New York City honors Tony's 90th birthday and musical legacy with a lighting ceremony

2017 Recipient of the Library of Congress' Gershwin Prize for Popular Song

2018 "I Left My Heart In San Francisco" is selected for inclusion into the National Recording Registry

2018 The City of San Francisco names the street outside the Fairmont Hotel "Tony Bennett Way"

LIBRARY OF CONGRESS

On the occasion of the Bicentennial of the Library of Congress we recognize

Tony Bennett
as a
Living Legend

for the lasting contribution you have made in enriching our national heritage.

James H. Billington
The Librarian of Congress
Washington, DC

GRAMMY® AWARDS

[All title genres are Traditional Pop unless noted]

1963 (5th Awards)
Record of the Year
I Left My Heart in San Francisco
(Genre: General)

Best Solo Vocal Performance, Male
I Left My Heart in San Francisco
(Genre: Pop)

1993 (35th Awards)
Best Traditional Pop Vocal Performance
Perfectly Frank

1994 (36th Awards)
Best Traditional Pop Vocal Performance
Steppin' Out

1995 (37th Awards)
Album of the Year
MTV Unplugged

Best Traditional Pop Vocal Performance
MTV Unplugged (Genre: General)

1997 (39th Awards)
Best Traditional Pop Vocal Performance
Here's to the Ladies

1998 (40th Awards)
Best Traditional Pop Vocal Performance
Tony Bennett on Holiday

2000 (42nd Awards)
Best Traditional Pop Vocal Performance
Bennett Sings Ellington: Hot & Cool

2001 (43rd Awards)
Lifetime Achievement Award

Tony Bennett was awarded the Living Legend Award by the Library of Congress in April 2000 for the "lasting contribution" he has "made in enriching our national heritage."

2003 (45th Awards)
Best Traditional Pop Vocal Album
Playin' with My Friends:
Bennett Sings the Blues

2004 (46th Awards)
Best Traditional Pop Vocal Album
A Wonderful World (with k.d.
lang)
(award shared with k.d. lang)

2006 (48th Awards)
Best Traditional Pop Vocal Album
The Art of Romance

2007 (49th Awards)
Best Pop Collaboration with Vocals
For Once in My Life (with
Stevie Wonder)
(award shared with Stevie
Wonder)

Best Traditional Pop Vocal Album
Duets: An American Classic

2012 (54th Awards)
Best Traditional Pop Vocal Album
Duets II

Best Pop Duo/Group
Performance
Body and Soul (with Amy
Winehouse)
(award shared with Amy
Winehouse)

2015 (57th Awards)
Best Traditional Pop Vocal Album
Cheek to Cheek (with Lady Gaga)
(award shared with Lady Gaga)

2016 (58th Awards)
Best Traditional Pop Vocal Album
The Silver Lining: The Songs of
Jerome Kern (with Bill Charlap)
(award shared with Bill Charlap)

2018 (60th Awards)
Best Traditional Pop Vocal Album
Tony Bennett Celebrates 90

DISCOGRAPHY

ALBUMS AND CDS

FIFTIES

July 1952
Because of You (Columbia)
Because of You

Boulevard of Broken Dreams
While We're Young
I Wanna Love
Once There Lived a Fool
The Valentino Tango
I Won't Cry Anymore
Cold, Cold Heart

February 1955
Cloud 7 (Columbia)
I Fall in Love Too Easily
My Baby Just Cares for Me
My Heart Tells Me
Old Devil Moon
Love Letters
My Reverie
Give Me the Simple Life
While the Music Plays On
I Can't Believe You're in Love
with Me
Darn That Dream

October 1955
Alone At Last (Columbia)
Sing, You Sinners
Somewhere Along the Way
Since My Love Has Gone
Stranger in Paradise
Here in My Heart
Please, Driver (Once Around
the Park Again)

ca. 1955–56
The Voice of Your Choice (UK Philips)
There'll Be No Teardrops Tonight
Take Me Back Again
Something's Gotta Give
Stranger in Paradise
Close Your Eyes
What Will I Tell My Heart?
Tell Me That You Love Me
How Can I Replace You?

March 1956
Because of You (Columbia)
Close Your Eyes
I Can't Give You Anything But
Love
Boulevard of Broken Dreams
Because of You
May I Never Love Again
Cinnamon Sinner

January 1957
Tony (Tony Bennett Showcase)
(Columbia)

It Had to Be You
You Can Depend on Me
I'm Just a Lucky So and So
Taking a Chance on Love
These Foolish Things
I Can't Give You Anything
But Love
Boulevard of Broken Dreams
I'll Be Seeing You
Always
Love Walked In
Lost in the Stars
Without a Song

December 1957
The Beat of My Heart (Columbia)
Let's Begin
Lullaby of Broadway
Let There Be Love
Love for Sale
Army Air Corps Song
Crazy Rhythm
The Beat of My Heart
So Beats My Heart for You
Blues in the Night
Lazy Afternoon
Let's Face the Music and Dance
Just One of Those Things

July 1958
Long Ago and Far Away
(Columbia)
It Could Happen to You
Every Time We Say Goodbye
Long Ago (And Far Away)
It Amazes Me
The Way You Look Tonight
Be Careful, It's My Heart
My Foolish Heart
Time After Time
Fools Rush In
A Cottage for Sale
Blue Moon
So Far

November 1958
A String of Hits, Record 1,
Compilation (Columbia)
Stranger in Paradise
Cold Heart
Because of You
Rags to Riches
Boulevard of Broken Dreams
Young and Warm and Wonderful
In the Middle of an Island
Ça, C'est l'Amour

Candido Camero, Billy Exiner, and Tony Bennett
perform at a Columbia Records press party, 1957.

Just in Time
There'll Be No Teardrops
Tonight
Anywhere I Wander
Sing, You Sinners

July 1959
Hometown, My Town (Columbia)
The Skyscraper Blues
Penthouse Serenade (When
We're Alone)
By Myself
I Cover the Waterfront
Love Is Here to Stay
The Party's Over

August 1959
Blue Velvet (Columbia)
Blue Velvet
I Won't Cry Anymore
Have a Good Time
Congratulations to Someone
Here Comes that Heartache
Again
While We're Young
Solitaire
My Heart Won't Say Goodbye
Until Yesterday
Funny Thing
May I Never Love Again
It's So Peaceful in the Country

September 1959

In Person! With Count Basie
(Columbia)
Just in Time
When I Fall in Love
Taking a Chance on Love
Without a Song
Fascinatin' Rhythm
Solitude
Pennies from Heaven
Lost in the Stars
Firefly
There Will Never Be Another
  You
Lullaby of Broadway
Ol' Man River

SIXTIES

February 1960

To My Wonderful One (Columbia)
Wonderful One
Till
September Song
Suddenly
I'm a Fool to Want You
We Mustn't Say Goodbye
Autumn Leaves
Laura
April in Paris
Speak Low
Tenderly
Last Night When We Were
  Young

July 1960

Alone Together (Columbia)
Alone Together
This Is All I Ask
Out of This World
Walk in the Country
I'm Always Chasing Rainbows
Poor Butterfly
After You've Been Gone
Gone with the Wind
It's MagicHow Long Has This
  Been Going On?
For Heaven's Sake

October 1960

A String of Hits, Record 2,
Compilation (Columbia)
Smile
You'll Never Get Away from Me

I Am
Put on a Happy Face
Love Look Away
I'll Bring You a Rainbow
Ask Anyone in Love
You Can't Love Them All
Baby Talk to Me
Firefly
The Night That Heaven Fell
Climb Ev'ry Mountain

November 1960

A String of Harold Arlen
(Columbia)
When the Sun Comes Out
Over the Rainbow
House of Flowers
Come Rain or Come Shine
For Every Man There's a Woman
Let's Fall in Love
Right as the Rain
It Was Written in the Stars
What Good Does It Do?
Fun to Be Fooled
This Time the Dream's on Me
I've Got the World on a String

1961

*Bennett & Basie: Strike Up the
Band* (Roulette)
Strike Up the Band
I Guess I'll Have to Change My
  Plans
Chicago
With Plenty of Money and You
Growing Pains
Life Is a Song
I've Grown Accustomed to Her
  Face
Jeepers Creepers
Anything Goes
Poor Little Rich Girl
Are You Having Any Fun?

February 1961

Tony Sings for Two (Columbia)
I Didn't Know What Time It Was
Bewitched
Nobody's Heart Belongs to Me
I'm Thru with Love
My Funny Valentine
The Man That Got Away
Where or When
A Sleepin' Bee
Happiness Is a Thing Called Joe
Mam'selle

Just Friends
Street of Dreams
Skylark (outtake on CD)

August 1961

My Heart Sings (Columbia)
Don't Worry 'Bout Me
Dancing in the Dark
I'm Coming, Virginia
My Heart Sings
It Never Was You
You Took Advantage of Me
Close Your Eyes
Stella by Starlight
More Than You Know
My Ship
Lover Man
Toot, Toot, Tootsie! (Goodbye)

March 1962

*Mr. Broadway: Tony's
Greatest Broadway Hits,*
Compilation (Columbia)
Just in Time
You'll Never Get Away from Me
Put on a Happy Face
Follow Me
Climb Ev'ry Mountain
Love Look Away
Comes Once in a Lifetime
The Party's Over (edited)
Baby Talk to Me
Begin the Beguine
Stranger in Paradise
Lazy Afternoon

June 1962

I Left My Heart in San Francisco
(Columbia)
I Left My Heart in San Francisco
Once Upon a Time
Tender Is the Night
Smile
Love for Sale
Taking a Chance on Love
Candy Kisses
Have I Told You Lately?
The Rules of the Road
Marry Young
I'm Always Chasing Rainbows
The Best Is Yet to Come

August 1962

Tony Bennett at Carnegie Hall
(Columbia)
Lullaby of Broadway

Just in Time
All the Things You Are
Stranger in Paradise
Love Is Here to Stay
Climb Ev'ry Mountain
Ol' Man River
It Amazes Me
Firefly
I Left My Heart in San Francisco
How About You/April in Paris
Solitude
I'm Just a Lucky So and So
Always
Anything Goes
Blue Velvet
Rags to Riches
Because of You
What Good Does It Do?
Lost in the Stars
One for My Baby
Lazy Afternoons
Sing, You Sinners
Love Look Away
Sometimes I'm Happy
My Heart Tells Me
De Glory Road

1963

Tony Bennett Meets Gene Krupa
(Sandy Hook)
Have I Told You Lately?
April in Paris
Just in Time
I Left My Heart in San Francisco
Sometimes I'm Happy
Small World Isn't It?
Sunday
Fascinatin' Rhythm

February 1963

I Wanna Be Around (Columbia)
The Good Life
If I Love Again
I Wanna Be Around
Love Look Away (UK only)
I've Got Your Number (US album)
Until I Met You
Let's Face the Music and Dance
If You Were Mine
I Will Live My Life for You
Someone to Love
It Was Me
Quiet Nights of Quiet Stars
  (Corcovado)

July 1963

This Is All I Ask (Columbia)
  Keep Smiling at Trouble
  Autumn in Rome
  True Blue Lou
  The Way That I Feel
  This Is All I Ask
  The Moment of Truth
  Got Her Off My Hands
  (But Can't Get Her Off My
    Mind)
  Sandy's Smile
  Long About Now
  Young and Foolish
  Tricks
  On the Other Side of the Tracks

January 1964

The Many Moods of Tony
(Columbia)
  The Little Boy
  When Joanna Loved Me
  A Taste of Honey
  Soon It's Gonna Rain
  The Kid's a Dreamer
  So Long, Big Time
  Don't Wait Too Long
  Caravan
  Spring in Manhattan
  I'll Be Around
  You've Changed
  Limehouse Blues

May 1964

When Lights Are Low (Columbia)
  Nobody Else But Me
  When Lights Are Low
  On Green Dolphin Street
  Ain't Misbehavin'
  It's a Sin to Tell a Lie
  I've Got Just About Everything
  Judy
  Oh! You Crazy Moon
  Speak Low
  It Had to Be You
  It Could Happen to You
  The Rules of the Road

November 1964

Who Can I Turn To? (Columbia)
  Who Can I Turn To?
  Wrap Your Troubles in Dreams
  There's a Lull in My Life
  Autumn Leaves
  I Walk a Little Faster

The Brightest Smile in Town
  I've Never Seen
  Between the Devil and the Deep
    Blue Sea
  Listen, Little Girl
  Got the Gate on the Golden Gate
  Waltz for Debbie
  The Best Thing to Be Is a Person

April 1965

If I Ruled the World: Tony Bennett
(Songs for the Jet Set) (Columbia)
  Song of the Jet
  Fly Me to the Moon (In Other
    Words)
  How Insensitive
  If I Ruled the World
  Love Scene
  My Ship (UK album)
  Take the Moment (US album)
  Then Was Then and Now Is Now
  Sweet Lorraine
  The Right to Love
  Watch What Happens
  All My Tomorrows
  Lazy Afternoon (UK album)
  Two by Two (US album)

July 1965

Tony Bennett's Greatest Hits,
Compilation (Columbia)
  I Left My Heart in San Francisco
  I Wanna Be Around
  Quiet Nights of Quiet Stars
    (Corcovado)
  When Joanna Loved Me
  The Moment of Truth
  Who Can I Turn To?
  The Good Life
  A Taste of Honey
  This Is All I Ask
  Once Upon a Time
  The Best Is Yet to Come
  If I Ruled the World

1965

The Oscar Soundtrack (CBS)
  The Theme from *The Oscar*
    (Maybe September)

January 1966

The Movie Song Album
(Columbia)
  The Theme from *The Oscar*
    (Maybe September)
  Girl Talk

The Gentle Rain
  Emily
  The Pawnbroker
  Samba de Orfeu
  The Shadow of Your Smile
  Smile
  The Second Time Around
  The Days of Wine and Roses
  Never Too Late
  The Trolley Song

August 1966

A Time for Love (Columbia)
  A Time for Love
  The Very Thought of You
  Trapped in the Web of Love
  My Funny Valentine
  In the Wee Small Hours of the
    Morning
  Yesterdays
  Georgia Rose
  The Shining Sea
  Sleepy Time Gal
  Touch the Earth
  I'll Only Miss Her When I Think
    of Her

March 1967

Tony Makes It Happen (Columbia)
  On the Sunny Side of the Street
  A Beautiful Friendship
  Don't Get Around Much
    Anymore
  What Makes It Happen?
  The Lady's in Love with You
  Can't Get Out of This Mood
  I Don't Know Why (I Just Do)
  I Let a Song Go Out of My Heart
  Country Girl
  Old Devil Moon
  She's Funny That Way

December 1967

For Once in My Life (Columbia)
  They Can't Take That Away
    from Me
  Something in Your Smile
  Days of Love
  Broadway/Crazy Rhythm/Lullaby
    of Broadway
  For Once in My Life
  Sometimes I'm Happy
  Out of This World
  Baby, Dream Your Dream
  How Do You Say Auf
    Wiedersehen?

Keep Smiling at Trouble
  (Trouble's a Bubble)

July 1968

Yesterday I Heard the Rain
(Columbia)
  Yesterday I Heard the Rain
  Hi-Ho
  Hushabye Mountain
  Home Is the Place
  Love Is Here to Stay
  Get Happy
  A Fool of Fools
  I Only Have Eyes for You
  Sweet Georgie Fame
  Only the Young
  There Will Never Be Another
    You

November 1968

Snowfall: The Tony Bennett
Christmas Album
(Columbia)
  Snowfall
  My Favorite Things
  The Christmas Song
  Medley: We Wish you a Merry
    Christmas/Silent Night, O
    Come, All Ye Faithful/ Jingle
    Bells, Where Is Love?
  Christmasland
  I Love the Winter Weather/ I've
    Got My Love to Keep Me
    Warm
  White Christmas
  Winter Wonderland
  Have Yourself a Merry Little
    Christmas
  I'll Be Home for Christmas (CD
    only)

April 1969

Greatest Hits Volume 2,
Compilation (Columbia)
  People
  For Once in My Life
  The Shadow of Your Smile
  Yesterday I Heard the Rain
  My Favorite Things
  Watch What Happens
  Fly Me to the Moon (In Other
    Words)
  How Insensitive (edited)
  Georgia Rose
  A Time for Love
  The Gentle Rain

July 1969

Just One of Those Things,
Compilation (Columbia)
Let's Begin
Lullaby of Broadway
Let There Be Love
Love for Sale
Crazy Rhythm
The Beat of My Heart
Blues in the Night
Lazy Afternoon
Let's Face the Music and Dance
Just One of Those Things

July 1969

I've Gotta Be Me (Columbia)
I've Gotta Be Me
Over the Sun
Play It Again, Sam
Alfie
What the World Needs Now Is
    Love
Baby, Don't You Quit Now
That Night
They All Laughed
A Lonely Place
Whoever You Are, I Love You
Theme from *Valley of the Dolls*

December 1969

Tony Sings the Great Hits of Today
(Columbia)
MacArthur Park
Something
The Look of Love
Here, There and Everywhere
Live for Life
Little Green Apples
Eleanor Rigby
My Cherie Amour
Is That All There Is?
Here
Sunrise, Sunset

SEVENTIES

ca. 1970

16 Most Requested Songs,
Compilation (Columbia)
Because of You
Stranger in Paradise
Rags to Riches
Boulevard of Broken Dreams
Cold, Cold Heart

Just in Time
I Left My Heart in San Francisco
I Wanna Be Around
Who Can I Turn To?
For Once in My Life
This Is All I Ask
Smile
Tender Is the Night
The Shadow of Your Smile
Love Story (Where Do I Begin)
The Good Life

October 1970

Something (Columbia)
Something
The Long and Winding Road
Everybody's Talkin'
On a Clear Day
Coco
Think How It's Gonna Be
Wave
Make It Easy on Yourself
Come Saturday Morning
When I Look in Your Eyes
Yellow Days
What a Wonderful World

December 1970

All-Time Hall of Fame Hits,
Compilation (Columbia)
Because of You
Cold, Cold Heart
Rags to Riches
One for My Baby/It Had to Be
    You
I Left My Heart in San Francisco
I Wanna Be Around
This Is All I Ask
The Good Life
The Shadow of Your Smile
Who Can I Turn To
Yesterday I Heard the Rain
For Once in My Life

January 1971

Get Happy Live with the
London Philharmonic Orchestra
(Columbia)
I Left My Heart in San Francisco
I Want to Be Happy
If I Ruled the World
Get Happy
Tea for Two
Let There Be Love
Love Story (Where Do I Begin)
The Trolley Song

I Left My Heart/I Wanna Be
    Around
Old Devil Moon
Country Girl
There Will Never Be Another
    You
Wave
On the Sunny Side of the Street
For Once in My Life
What the World Needs Now Is
    Love
I'll Begin Again
Closing Theme—San Francisco

February 1971

Love Story (Columbia)
Love Story (Where Do I Begin)
Tea for Two
I Want to Be Happy
Individual Thing
I Do Not Know a Day I Did Not
    Love You
They Can't Take That Away
    from Me
When Joanna Loved Me
Country Girl
The Gentle Rain
Soon It's Gonna Rain
A Taste of Honey
I'll Begin Again

February 1971

Love Songs, Double Compilation
(CBS)
Alone Together
Bewitched
The Very Thought of You
Tender Is the Night
I Only Have Eyes for You
Where or When
Laura
Penthouse Serenade
I Cover the Waterfront
Stella by Starlight
Tenderly
I'm Thru with Love
September Song
My Funny Valentine
The Days of Wine and Roses
Street of Dreams
The Second Time Around
It Had to Be You
Till
Love for Sale

August 1971

The Very Thought of You,
Compilation (Columbia)
Just in Time
Don't Get Around Much
    Anymore
The Very Thought of You
Stranger in Paradise
The Second Time Around
Stella by Starlight
It's Magic
Laura
If I Love Again
I'll Be Around

1972

Tony Bennett's Greatest Hits No. 7
(MGM Verve)
My Love
'O Sole Mio
The Good Things in Life
Cute
Mimi
London by Night
On the Sunny Side of the Street
Let's Do It
Sophisticated Lady
Living Together, Growing
    Together
Tell Her It's Snowing (Short
    Version)
Give Me Love

1972

The Good Things in Life (MGM
Verve)
The Good Things in Life
'O Sole Mio
Passing Strangers
End of a Love Affair
Oh! Lady Be Good
Blues for Breakfast
Mimi
Invitation
Someone to Light up My Life
It Was You
Cute
The Midnight Sun
London by Night
The Good Things in Life
    (Closing)

January 1972

Summer of '42, Compilation
(Columbia)
The Summer Knows

Walk About
It Was Me
I'm Losing My Mind
Till
Somewhere Along the Line
Coffee Break
More and More
Irena
My Inamorata
The Shining Sea

May 1972
With Love (Columbia)
Here's That Rainy Day
Remind Me
How Beautiful Is Night (With You)
Maybe This Time
The Riviera
Street of Dreams
Love
Twilight World
Lazy Day
Easy Come, Easy Go
Harlem Butterfly
Dream

August 1972
All-Time Greatest Hits (Columbia)
Something
Love Story (Where Do I Begin)
Maybe This Time
Just in Time
For Once in My Life
I Left My Heart in San Francisco
Because of You
Boulevard of Broken Dreams
Stranger in Paradise
I Wanna Be Around
A Time for Love
Who Can I Turn To?
This Is All I Ask
Smile
Sing, You Sinners
Firefly
The Shadow of Your Smile
Put on a Happy Face
Love Look Away
Rags to Riches

March 1973
Tony! Compilation (Columbia)
Who Can I Turn To?
Yellow Days
Smile
Alfie

The Look of Love
Something
There's a Lull in My Life
MacArthur Park
I'll Only Miss Her When I Think of Her
The Second Time Around

1973
Listen Easy (Philips)
Love Is the Thing
Rain, Rain (Don't Go Away)
The Hands of Time
I Concentrate on You
At Long Last Love
If I Could Go Back
On the Sunny Side of the Street
The Garden (Once in a Garden)
My Funny Valentine
How Little We Know
Tell Her That It's Snowing

June 1973
Sunrise, Sunset, Compilation (Columbia)
The Days of Wine and Roes
Climb Ev'ry Mountain
Yesterdays
She's Funny That Way
You'll Never Get Away from Me
Sunrise, Sunset
Love Story (Where Do I Begin)
The Party's Over
Put on a Happy Face
Begin the Beguine
Don't Get Around Much Anymore

September 1973
Tony Bennett Sings 10 Rodgers & Hart Songs (Improv)
This Can't Be Love
Blue Moon
The Lady Is a Tramp
Lover
Manhattan
Spring Is Here
Have You Met Miss Jones?
Isn't It Romantic?
Wait Till You See Her
I Could Write a Book

September 1973
Tony Bennett Sings More Great Rodgers & Hart (Improv)
Thou Swell
The Most Beautiful Girl in the World
There's a Small Hotel
I've Got Five Dollars
You Took Advantage of Me
Wish I Were in Love Again
This Funny World
My Heart Stood Still
My Romance
Mountain Greenery

1974
The Trolley Song, Compilation (Embassy)
Alfie
The Days of Wine and Roses
There Will Never Be Another You
What the World Needs Now Is Love
A Beautiful Friendship
She's Funny That Way
Fascinatin' Rhythm
Old Devil Moon
I've Gotta Be Me

Girl Talk
The Trolley Song

1974
When I Fall in Love, Compilation (Hallmark)
When I Fall in Love
Taking a Chance on Love
Pennies from Heaven
Ol' Man River
Play It Again, Sam
They All Laughed
The Gentle Rain
Firefly
How About You?
April in Paris
Solitude
Country Girl

June 1975
The Golden Touch of Tony Bennett, Compilation (Columbia)
I Left My Heart in San Francisco
Just in Time
Blue Velvet
A Taste of Honey
Cold, Cold Heart
For Once in My Life
This Is All I Ask
Rags to Riches

Cello Case and Mic Stand, drawing *by Tony Bennett.*

If I Ruled the World

In the Middle of an Island

Smile

Don't Wait Too Long

Can You Find It in Your Heart?

One for My Baby

Stranger in Paradise

Fly Me to the Moon (In Other Words)

My Funny Valentine

Climb Ev'ry Mountain

Spring in Manhattan

I Wanna Be Around

The Good Life

Solitaire

The Shadow of Your Smile

Here in My Heart

Who Can I Turn To?

ca. 1975
Spotlight on . . . Tony Bennett, Compilation (Philips)

End of a Love Affair

Passing Strangers

All That Love Went to Waste

Love Is the Thing

On the Sunny Side of the Street

The Garden (Once in a Garden)

Invitation

Someone to Light Up My Life

If I Could Go Back

The Hands of Time

'O Sole Mio

Some of These Days

The Midnight Sun

It Was You

London by Night

My Love

Oh! Lady Be Good

Cute

I Concentrate on You

Mimi

Tell Her That It's Snowing

Blues for Breakfast

At Long Last Love

My Funny Valentine

How Little We Know

Rain, Rain (Don't Go Away)

The Good Things in Life

Give Me Love, Give Me Peace

1975
The Tony Bennett/Bill Evans Album (Fantasy)

Young and Foolish

The Touch of Your Lips

Some Other Time

When in Rome

We'll Be Together Again

My Foolish Heart

Waltz for Debbie

But Beautiful

The Days of Wine and Roses

1975
*Tony Bennett Sings "Life Is Beautiful"** (Improv)

Life Is Beautiful

All Mine

Bridges

Reflections

Experiment

This Funny World

As Time Goes By

I Used to Be Color Blind

Lost in the Stars

There'll Be Some Changes Made

*Additional songs for 2003 Concord Release: Cole Porter Medley: What Is This Thing Called Love / Love for Sale/ I'm in Love Again / You'd Be So Nice to Come Home To / Easy to Love / It's Alright with Me / Night and Day / Dream Dancing / I've Got You Under My Skin/ Get Out of Town / What Is This Thing Called Love (reprise)

May 1975
Tony Bennett Sings, Compilation (Columbia)

Fly Me to the Moon (In Other Words)

Who Can I Turn To?

If I Ruled the World

The Trolley Song

Sweet Lorraine

My Favorite Things

Candy Kisses

Put on a Happy Face

A Taste of Honey

Country Girl

They Can't Take That Away from Me

Climb Ev'ry Mountain

May 1975
Let's Fall in Love with the Songs of Harold Arlen and Cy Coleman, Compilation (Columbia)

When the Sun Comes Out

House of Flowers

Come Rain or Come Shine

Let's Fall in Love

Over the Rainbow

Right As the Rain

It Was Written in the Stars

Fun to Be Fooled

This Time the Dream's on Me

I've Got the World on a String

I've Got Your Number

On the Other Side of the Tracks

Firefly

The Rules of the Road

The Riviera

The Best Is Yet to Come

I Walk a Little Faster

It Amazes Me

Baby, Dream Your Dream

Then Was Then, and Now Is Now

1976
At Long Last Love, Compilation (Philips)

Someone to Light up My Life

At Long Last Love

How Little We Know

It Was You

Passing Strangers

If I Could Go Back

End of Love Affair

My Love

I Concentrate on You

'O Sole Mio

The Midnight Sun

Living Together, Growing Together

1977
Tony Bennett & Bill Evans Together Again (Improv)

The Bad and the Beautiful

Lucky to Be Me

Make Someone Happy

The Two Lonely People

A Child Is Born

You're Nearer

You Don't Know What Love Is

Maybe September

Lonely Girl

You Must Believe in Spring

May 1977
The McPartlands and Friends Make Magnificent Music (Improv)

Watch What Happens

While We're Young

In a Mellow Tone

'S Wonderful/I Left My Heart in San Francisco

ca. 1977
Stage and Screen Hits, Compilation (DBM)

Cole Porter 10-Song Medley

Experiment

One

This Funny World

Lost in the Stars

As Time Goes By

I Used to Be Color Blind

Mr. Magic

The Most Beautiful Girl in the World

There's a Small Hotel

I've Got Five Dollars

I Wish I Were in Love Again

Manhattan

The Lady Is a Tramp

My Romance

Mountain Greenery

Lucky to Be Me

Make Someone Happy

You're Nearer

You Don't Know What Love Is

Lonely Girl

You Must Believe in Spring

ca. 1978
The Unforgettable Tony Bennett, Compilation (Castle)

There'll Be Some Changes Made

Blue Moon

The Lady Is a Tramp

Lover

Manhattan

I Could Write a Book

Spring Is Here

A Child Is Born

Make Someone Happy

Life Is Beautiful

Maybe September

Lonely Girl

You Don't Know What Love Is

Thou Swell

There's a Small Hotel

As Time Goes By

EIGHTIES

May 1986

The Art of Excellence (Columbia)
Why Do People Fall in Love?
Moments Like This
What Are You Afraid Of?
When Love Was All We Had
So Many Stars
Everybody Has the Blues
How Do You Keep the Music Playing?
City of the Angels
Forget the Woman
A Rainy Day
I Got Lost in Her Arms
The Day You Leave Me

March 1987

Tony Bennett/Jazz, Compilation (Columbia)
I Can't Believe You're in Love with Me
Don't Get Around Much Anymore
Stella by Starlight
On Green Dolphin Street
Let's Face the Music and Dance
I'm Through with Love
Solitude
Lullaby of Broadway
Dancing in the Dark
I Let a Song Go Out of My Heart
When the Lights Are Low
Just One of Those Things
Crazy Rhythm
Judy
Give Me the Simple Life
Street of Dreams
Love Scene
While the Music Plays On
Close Your Eyes
Out of This World

October 1987

Bennett/Berlin (Columbia)
They Say It's Wonderful
Isn't This a Lovely Day?
All of My Life
Now It Can Be Told
The Song Is Ended
When I Lost You
Cheek to Cheek
Let Yourself Go

Let's Face the Music and Dance
Shakin' the Blues Away
Russian Lullaby
White Christmas

December 1989

Astoria: Portrait of the Artist (Columbia)
When Do the Bells Ring for Me?
I Was Lost, I Was Drifting
A Little Street Where Old Friends Meet
The Girl I Love
It's Like Reaching for the Moon
Speak Low
The Folks Who Live on the Hill
Antonia
A Weaver of Dreams/ There Will Never Be Another You
Body and Soul
Where Do You Go from Love?
The Boulevard of Broken Dreams
Where Did the Magic Go?
I've Come Home Again

NINETIES

1991

Forty Years: The Artistry of Tony Bennett, 4-CD Compilation (Columbia)

DISC ONE:
The Boulevard of Broken Dreams
Because of You
Cold, Cold Heart
Blue Velvet
Rags to Riches
Stranger in Paradise
While the Music Plays On
May I Never Love Again
Sing, You Sinners
Just in Time
Lazy Afternoon
Ça, C'est l'Amour
I Get a Kick Out of You
It Amazes Me
Penthouse Serenade
Lost in the Stars
Lullaby of Broadway
Firefly
A Sleepin' Bee

The Man That Got Away
Skylark
September Song
Till

DISC TWO:
Begin the Beguine
Put on a Happy Face
The Best Is Yet to Come
This Time the Dream's on Me
Close Your Eyes
Toot, Toot, Tootsie! (Goodbye)
Dancing in the Dark
Stella by Starlight
Tender Is the Night
Once Upon a Time
I Left My Heart in San Francisco
Until I Met You
If I Love Again
I Wanna Be Around
The Good Life
It Was Me
Spring in Manhattan
The Moment of Truth
This Is All I Ask
A Taste of Honey
When Joanna Loved Me
I'll Be Around

DISC THREE:
Nobody Else But Me
It Had to Be You
I've Got Just About Everything
Who Can I Turn To?
Waltz for Debbie
I Walk a Little Faster
Wrap Your Troubles in Dreams
If I Ruled the World
Fly Me to the Moon (In Other Words)
Love Scene
Sweet Lorraine
The Shadow of Your Smile
I'll Only Miss Her When I Think of Her
Baby, Dream Your Dream
Smile
Song from *The Oscar* (Maybe September)
Emily
The Very Thought of You
A Time for Love
Country Girl

DISC FOUR:
Days of Love
Keep Smiling at Trouble
For Once in My Life
Who Cares (So Long as You Care for Me)
Hi-Ho
Baby, Don't You Quit Now
Something
I Do Not Know a Day I Did Not Love You
Old Devil Moon
Remind Me
Maybe This Time
Some Other Time
My Foolish Heart
But Beautiful
How Do You Keep the Music Playing?
What Are You Afraid Of?
Why Do People Fall in Love?/ People
I Got Lost in Her Arms
When I Lost You
Shakin' the Blues Away
Antonia
When Do the Bells Ring for Me?

1992

Perfectly Frank (Columbia)
Time After Time
I Fall in Love Too Easily
East of the Sun (West of the Moon)
Nancy
I Thought About You
Night and Day
I've Got the World on a String
I'm Glad There Is You
A Nightingale Sang in Berkeley Square
I Wished on the Moon
You Go to My Head
The Lady Is a Tramp
I See Your Face Before Me
Day In, Day Out
Indian Summer
Call Me Irresponsible
Here's That Rainy Day
Last Night When We Were Young
I Wish I Were in Love Again
A Foggy Day
Don't Worry 'Bout Me
One for My Baby

Angel Eyes
I'll Be Seeing You

October 1993
Steppin' Out (Columbia)
Steppin' Out with My Baby
Who Cares?
Top Hat, White Tie and Tails
They Can't Take That Away
     from Me
Dancing in the Dark
Shine on Your Shoes
He Loves and She Loves
They All Laughed
I Concentrate on You
You're All the World to Me
All of You
Nice Work If You Can Get It
It Only Happens When I Dance
     with You
Shall We Dance?
You're So Easy to Dance With/
     Change Partners/Cheek to
     Cheek
I Guess I'll Have to Change My
     Plans
That's Entertainment
By Myself

June 1994
MTV Unplugged (Columbia)
Old Devil Moon
Speak Low
It Had to Be You
I Love a Piano
It Amazes Me
The Girl I Love
Fly Me to the Moon
You're All the World to Me
Rags to Riches
When Joanna Loved Me
The Good Life/I Wanna Be
     Around
I Left My Heart in San Francisco
Steppin' Out with My Baby
Moonglow (duet with k.d. lang)
They Can't Take That Away
     from Me (duet with Elvis
     Costello)
A Foggy Day
All of You
Body and Soul
It Don't Mean a Thing (If It
     Ain't Got That Swing)
Autumn Leaves/Indian Summer

October 1995
Here's to the Ladies (Columbia)
People
I'm in Love Again
Somewhere Over the Rainbow
My Love Went to London
Poor Butterfly
Sentimental Journey
Cloudy Morning
Tenderly
Down in the Depths
Moonlight in Vermont
Tangerine
God Bless the Child
Daybreak
You Showed Me the Way
Honeysuckle Rose
Maybe This Time
I Got Rhythm
My Ideal

February 1997
Tony Bennett on Holiday
(Columbia)
Solitude
All of Me
When a Woman Loves a Man
Me, Myself and I (Are All in
     Love with You)
She's Funny That Way (I Got a
     Woman,
Crazy for Me)
If I Could Be with You (One
     Hour Tonight)
Willow Weep for Me
Laughing at Life
I Wished on the Moon
What a Little Moonlight Can Do
My Old Flame
The Ole Devil Called Love
Ill Wind (You're Blowing Me No
     Good)
These Foolish Things (Remind
     Me of You)
Some Other Spring
Crazy She Calls Me
Good Morning, Heartache
Trav'lin' Light
God Bless the Child
     (duet with Billie Holiday)

September 1998
The Playground (RPM/Sony
Wonder)
The Playground

Ac-Cent-Tchu-Ate the Positive
Dat Dere
Little Things (duet with Elmo)
Put on a Happy Face (duet with
     Rosie O'Donnell)
Because We're Kids
My Mom
Swinging on a Star
Bein' Green (duet with Kermit
     the Frog)
When You Wish Upon a Star
(It's Only) A Paper Moon
The Inch Worm
The Bare Necessities
Make the World Your Own
All God's Chillun Got Rhythm

September 1999
*Tony Bennett Sings Ellington: Hot
& Cool* (RPM/Columbia)
Do Nothin' Till You Hear from
     Me
Mood Indigo
She's Got It Bad (And That
     Ain't Good)
Caravan
Chelsea Bridge
Azure
I'm Just a Lucky So and So
In a Sentimental Mood
Don't Get Around Much
     Anymore
Sophisticated Lady
In a Mellow Tone
Day Dream
Prelude to a Kiss
It Don't Mean a Thing (If It
     Ain't Got That Swing)

**TWENTY-FIRST
CENTURY**

2000
The Ultimate Tony Bennett,
Compilation (RPM/Columbia)
I Left My Heart in San Francisco
Because of You
Rags to Riches
Just in Time
Stranger in Paradise
The Boulevard of Broken
     Dreams
I Wanna Be Around
The Good Life

The Shadow of Your Smile
Put on a Happy Face
If I Ruled the World
Smile
Night and Day
How Do You Keep the Music
     Playing?
Mood Indigo
Blue Velvet
Steppin' Out with My Baby
When Joanna Loved Me
When Do the Bells Ring for Me?
The Best Is Yet to Come

November 2001
*Playin' with My Friends: Bennett
Sings the Blues* (RPM/Columbia)
Alright, Okay, You Win
     (duet with Diana Krall)
Everyday (I Have the Blues)
     (duet with Stevie Wonder)
Don't Cry Baby
Good Morning, Heartache
     (duet with Sheryl Crow)
Let the Good Times Roll
     (duet with B. B. King)
Evenin' (duet with Ray Charles)
     I Gotta Right to Sing the
     Blues (duet with Bonnie
     Raitt)
Keep the Faith, Baby (duet with
     k.d. lang)
Old Count Basie Is Gone
Blue and Sentimental (duet with
     Kay Starr)
New York State of Mind
     (duet with Billy Joel)
Undecided Blues
Blues in the Night
Stormy Weather (duet with
     Natalie Cole)
Playin' with My Friends
     (duet with various artists)

2002
The Essential Tony Bennett
(Columbia/RPM)

DISC ONE:
Because of You
Cold, Cold Heart
Blue Velvet
Rags to Riches
Stranger in Paradise
Sing, You Sinners

The Boulevard of Broken
     Dreams
Just in Time
It Amazes Me
Love Look Away
Lost in the Stars
Firefly
Put on a Happy Face
The Best Is Yet to Come
Tender Is the Night
Once Upon a Time
I Left My Heart in San Francisco
I Wanna Be Around
The Good Life
This Is All I Ask
When Joanna Loved Me
The Rules of the Road

Who Can I Turn To? (When
     Nobody Needs Me)
If I Ruled the World
Fly Me to the Moon
The Shadow of Your Smile
Smile
The Very Thought of You
For Once in My Life
Yesterday I Heard the Rain
My Favorite Things
I Do Not Know a Day I Did Not
     Love You
Maybe This Time
How Do You Keep the Music
     Playing?
When Do the Bells Ring for Me?
Night and Day
Last Night When We Were
     Young
Steppin' Out with My Baby
It Don't Mean a Thing
     (If It Ain't Got That Swing)
Mood Indigo
Keep the Faith, Baby (duet with
     k.d. lang)

November 2002
*A Wonderful World** (RPM/
     Columbia)
Exactly Like You
La Vie en Rose
I'm Confessin' (That I Love
     You)
You Can Depend on Me
What a Wonderful World
That's My Home

A Kiss to Build a Dream On
I Wonder
Dream a Little Dream of Me
You Can't Lose a Broken Heart
That Lucky Old Sun
     (Just Rolls Around Heaven
     All Day)
If We Never Meet Again

*All are duets with k.d. lang.

2004
*Fifty Years: The Artistry of Tony
Bennett*, 5-CD Compilation/
Boxed Set (Columbia/Legacy)

DISC ONE:
The Boulevard of Broken
     Dreams
Because of You
Cold, Cold Heart
Blue Velvet
Rags to Riches
Stranger in Paradise
While the Music Plays On
May I Never Love Again
Sing, You Sinners
Just in Time
Lazy Afternoon
Ça, C'est l'Amour
I Get a Kick Out of You
It Amazes Me
Penthouse Serenade (When
     We're Alone)
Lost in the Stars
Lullaby of Broadway
Firefly
A Sleepin' Bee
The Man That Got Away
Skylark
September Song
Till

DISC TWO
Begin the Beguine
Put on a Happy Face
The Best Is Yet to Come
This Time the Dream's on Me
Close Your Eyes
Toot, Toot, Tootsie! (Goodbye)
Dancing in the Dark
Stella by Starlight
Tender Is the Night
Once Upon a Time
I Left My Heart in San Francisco
Until I Met You

If I Love Again
I Wanna Be Around
The Good Life
It Was Me
Spring in Manhattan
The Moment of Truth
This Is All I Ask
A Taste of Honey
When Joanna Loved Me
I'll Be Around

DISC THREE:
Nobody Else But Me
It Had to Be You
I've Got Just About Everything
Who Can I Turn To? (When
     Nobody
     Needs Me)
Waltz for Debby
I Walk a Little Faster
Wrap Your Troubles in Dreams
     (And Dream Your Troubles
     Away)
If I Ruled the World
Fly Me to the Moon (In Other
     Words)
Love Scene
Sweet Lorraine
The Shadow of Your Smile
I'll Only Miss Her When I Think
     of Her
Baby, Dream Your Dream
Smile
Song from The Oscar (Maybe
     September)
Emily
The Very Thought of You
A Time for Love
Country Girl
Days of Love

DISC FOUR
Keep Smiling at Trouble
     (Trouble's a Bubble)
For Once in My Life
Who Cares? (So Long As You
     Care for Me)
Hi-Ho
Baby, Don't You Quit Now
Something
Cold, Cold Heart
I Do Not Know a Day I Did Not
     Love You
Old Devil Moon (Live)
Remind Me

Maybe This Time
Some Other Time
My Foolish Heart
But Beautiful
How Do You Keep the Music
     Playing?
What Are You Afraid Of
Why Do People Fall in Love?/
     People
I Got Lost in Her Arms
Shakin' the Blues Away
Antonia
When Do the Bells Ring for Me?

DISC FIVE:
East of the Sun (West of the
     Moon)
New York, New York
Steppin' Out with My Baby
They All Laughed
They Can't Take That Away
     from Me
Speak Low (Live)
Solitude
I Wished on the Moon
When a Woman Loves a Man
That Ole Devil Called Love
The Way You Look Tonight
Ac-Cent-Tchu-Ate the Positive
Bein' Green
Mood Indigo
Day Dream
Azure
Sophisticated Lady
Alright, Okay, You Win
Let the Good Times Roll
Evenin'
La Vie en Rose
What a Wonderful World

November 2004
The Art of Romance (RPM/
Columbia)
Close Enough for Love
All in Fun
Where Do You Start?
Little Did I Dream
I Remember You
Time to Smile
All for You
The Best Man
Don't Like Goodbyes
Being Alive
Gone with the Wind

September 2006

Duets: An American Classic (RPM/Columbia)

Lullaby of Broadway (duet with the Dixie Chicks)

Smile (duet with Barbra Streisand)

Put on a Happy Face (duet with James Taylor)

The Very Thought of You (duet with Paul McCartney)

The Shadow of Your Smile (duet with Juanes)

Rags to Riches (duet with Elton John)

The Good Life (duet with Billy Joel)

Cold, Cold Heart (duet with Tim McGraw)

If I Ruled the World (duet with Celine Dion)

The Best Is Yet to Come (duet with Diana Krall)

For Once in My Life (duet with Stevie Wonder)

Are You Havin' Any Fun? (duet with Elvis Costello)

Because of You (duet with k.d. lang)

Just in Time (duet with Michael Bublé)

The Boulevard of Broken Dreams (duet with Sting)

I Wanna Be Around (duet with Bono)

Sing, You Sinners (duet with John Legend)

I Left My Heart in San Francisco (piano accompaniment by Bill Charlap)

How Do You Keep the Music Playing? (duet with George Michael)

October 2008

A Swingin' Christmas, Featuring the Count Basie Big Band (RPM/Columbia)

I'll Be Home for Christmas

Silver Bells

All I Want for Christmas Is You

My Favorite Things

Christmas Time Is Here

Winter Wonderland

Have Yourself a Merry Little Christmas

Santa Claus Is Coming to Town

I've Got My Love to Keep Me Warm (duet with Antonia Bennett)

The Christmas Waltz

O Christmas Tree

September 2011

Duets II (RPM/Columbia)

The Lady Is a Tramp (duet with Lady Gaga)

One For My Baby (And One More For The Road) (duet with John Mayer)

Body and Soul (duet with Any Winehouse)

Don't Get Around Much Anymore (duet with Michael Bublé)

Blue Velvet (duet with k.d lang)

How Do You Keep the Music Playing (duet with Aretha Franklin)

The Girl I Love (duet with Sheryl Crow)

On The Sunny Side of the Street (duet with Willie Nelson)

Who Can I Turn To (When Nobody Needs Me) (duet with Queen Latifah)

Speak Low (duet with Norah Jones)

This Is All I Ask (duet with John Groban)

Watch What Happens (duet with Natalie Cole)

Stranger in Paradise (duet with Andrea Bocelli)

The Way You Look Tonight (duet with Faith Hill)

Yesterday I Heard the Rain (duet with Alejandro Sanz)

It Had to Be You (duet with Carrie Underwood)

When Do the Bells Ring for Me (duet with Mariah Carey)

October 2011

The Classic Christmas Album (RPM/Columbia/Legacy)

Santa Claus Is Coming to Town

My Favorite Things

Christmas Time Is Here

Deck the Halls

The First Noel (duet with Plácido Domingo)

The Christmas Song (Chestnuts Roasting on an Open Fire)

Silver Bells

Have Yourself a Merry Little Christmas

O Little Town of Bethlehem

I Love the Winter Weather

I've Got My Love to Keep Me Warm (duet with Antonia Bennett)

Christmas in Herald Square

I'll Be Home for Christmas

O Come All Ye Faithful

What Child Is This

Winter Wonderland

Silent Night

White Christmas

October 2012

Viva Duets (RPM/Columbia)

The Best Is Yet to Come (duet with Chayanne)

The Way You Look Tonight (duet with Thalía)

Steppin' Out With My Baby (duet with Christina Aguilera)

For Once in My Life (duet with Marc Anthony)

Are You Havin' Any Fun? (duet with Dani Martín)

Blue Velvet (duet with Maria Gadú)

The Good Life (with Franco De Vita)

I Wanna Be Around (with Ricardo Arjona)

Who Can I Turn To (When Nobody Needs Me) (duet with Gloria Estefan)

Don't Get Around Much Anymore (duet with Miguel Bosé)

The Very Thought of You (duet with Ana Carolina)

Just on Time (duet with Juan Luis Guerra)

Cold, Cold Heart (duet with Vicentico)

Rags to Riches (duet with Romeo Santos)

Return to Me (Regresa a Mí) (with Vicente Fernández)

May 2013

Bennett/Brubeck: The White House Sessions, Live 1962 (RPM/Columbia/Legacy)

Introduction

Take Five

Band Introduction

Nomad

Thank You (Djiekuje)

Castilian Blues

Introduction

Just in Time

Small World

Make Someone Happy

Rags to Riches

One for My Baby (And One More for the Road)

I Left My Heart in San Francisco

Lullaby of Broadway

Chicago (That Toddlin' Town)

That Old Black Magic

There Will Never Be Another You

October 2013

Tony Bennett Live at the Sahara: Las Vegas 1964 (RPM/Columbia/Legacy)

Overture: The Moment of Truth

This Could Be the Start of Something Big

It's a Sin to Tell a Lie

Ain't Misbehavin'

Rags to Riches

Keep Smiling at Trouble (Trouble's A Bubble)

Time after Time

Sing You Sinners

One for My Baby (And One More for the Road)

The Rules of the Road

One for My Baby (And One More for the Road) (reprise)

Ma'selle

From This Moment On

Comedy Routine with Milton Berle, Danny Thomas & Mickey Rooney

I'm Way Ahead of the Game

Quiet Nights of Quiet Stars (Corcovado)

Firefly

Once Upon a Time

Tony Bennett, August 5, 2015..

Lullaby of Broadway
Chicago (That Toddlin' Town)
I Left My Heart in San Francisco
I Wanna Be Around
I Left My Heart in San Francisco (reprise)
Finale: The Moment of Truth

January 2014

The Classics (RPM/Columbia/ Legacy)

DISC ONE:

The Boulevard of Broken Dreams (Gigolo and Gigolette)
Because of You
Cold, Cold Heart
Blue Velvet
Rags to Riches
Stranger in Paradise
Just in Time
The Way You Look Tonight
Put on a Happy Face
I Left My Heart in San Francisco
I Wanna Be Around
The Good Life
Who Can I Turn To (When Nobody Needs Me)
If I Ruled the World
My Favorite Things

How Do You Keep the Music Playing?
When Do the Bells Ring for Me?

DISC TWO:

New York, New York (duet with Frank Sinatra)
Evenin' (duet with Ray Charles)
What a Wonderful World (duet with k.d lang)
Smile (duet with Barbra Streisand)
The Shadow of Your Smile (duet with Juanes)
The Best Is Yet to Come (duet with Diana Krall)
For Once in My Life (duet with Stevie Wonder)
One for My Baby (And One More for the Road) (duet with John Mayer)
Don't Get Around Much Anymore (duet with Michael Bublé)
The Lady Is a Tramp (duet with Lady Gaga)
Body and Soul (duet with Amy Winehouse)
It Had To Be You (duet with Carrie Underwood)

Steppin' Out With My Baby (duet with Christina Aguilera)

September 2014

Cheek to Cheek* (Streamline Records/Columbia/RPM/ Interscope Records)

Anything Goes
Cheek to Cheek
Nature Boy
I Can't Give You Anything But Love
I Won't Dance
Firefly
Lush Life (Lady Gaga Solo)
Sophisticated Lady (Tony Bennett Solo)
Let's Face the Music and Dance
But Beautiful
It Don't Mean a Thing (If It Ain't Got That Swing)

*All are duets with Lady Gaga except when noted

September 2015

Tony Bennett & Bill Charlap: The Silver Lining—The Songs of Jerome Kern (RPM / Columbia)

All The Things You Are
Pick Yourself Up
The Last Time I Saw Paris
I Won't Dance
Long Ago and Far Away
Dearly Beloved
The Song Is You
They Didn't Believe Me
I'm Old Fashioned
The Way You Look Tonight
Yesterdays
Make Believe
Nobody Else But Me
Look for the Silver Lining

December 2016

Tony Bennett Celebrates 90 (RPM / Columbia)

The Lady Is a Tramp (Lady Gaga)
The Good Life (Michael Bublé)
Ave Maria (Andrea Bocelli)
The Very Thought of You / If I Ruled the World (Kevin Spacey)

I've Got the World on a String (Diana Krall)
New York State of Mind (Tony Bennett and Billy Joel)
I Can't Give You Anything But Love (Rufus Wainwright)
A Kiss to Build a Dream On (k.d lang)
Visions (Stevie Wonder)
La Vie en Rose (Lady Gaga)
Can You Feel the Love Tonight (Elton John)
Autumn Leaves (Leslie Odom Jr.)
Who Cares? (Tony Bennett)
The Best Is Yet to Come (Tony Bennett)
I Left My Heart in San Francisco (Tony Bennett)
I Got Rhythm (Tony Bennett)
How Do You Keep the Music Playing? (Tony Bennett)
Happy Birthday (Stevie Wonder)

September 2018

Love Is Here to Stay—Tony Bennett/ Diana Krall (Verve/Columbia)

'S Wonderful
My One and Only
But Not for Me
Nice Work If You Can Get It
Love Is Here to Stay
I Got Rhythm
Somebody Loves Me
Do It Again
I've Got a Crush on You
Fascinating Rhythm
They Can't Take That Away from Me
Who Cares?

SINGLES

1950

Boulevard of Broken Dreams
Don't Cry, Baby
I Can't Give You Anything but Love
I Wanna Be Loved
Just Say I Love Her
Kiss You
Let's Make Love
One Lie Leads to Another
Our Lady of Fatima
Sing, You Sinners

1951
Beautiful Madness
Because of You
Blue Velvet
Cold, Cold Heart
I Won't Cry Anymore
Once There Lived a Fool
Silly Dreamer
Since My Love Has Gone
Solitaire
Valentino Tango
While We're Young

1952
Anywhere I Wander
Congratulations to Someone
Have a Good Time
Here in My Heart
I'm Lost Again
Please, My Love
Roses of Yesterday
Sleepless
Somewhere Along the Way
Stay Where You Are

Take Me
You Could Make Me Smile
    Again

1953
Here Comes That Heartache
    Again
I'll Go
I'm the King of Broken Hearts
No One Will Ever Know
Rags to Riches
Someone Turned the Moon
    Upside Down
Stranger in Paradise
Why Did It Have to Be Me?

1954
Cinnamon Sinner
Funny Thing
Madonna, Madonna
My Heart Won't Say Goodbye
Not As a Stranger
Please, Driver
Shoo-Gah (My Pretty Sugar)
Take Me Back Again

There'll Be No Teardrops Tonight
Until Yesterday

1955
Afraid of the Dark
Close Your Eyes
    (Come Back and) Tell Me
    That You Love Me
Come Next Spring
Don't Tell Me Why
Heart
How Can I Replace You?
It's Too Soon to Know
May I Never Love Again
Punch and Judy Love
What Will I Tell My Heart?
Whatever Lola Wants

1956
Can You Find It in Your Heart?
Capri in May
Forget Her
From the Candy Store on the
    Corner (to the Chapel on
    the Hill)

Happiness Street (Corner
    Sunshine Square)
Just in Time
The Autumn Waltz

1957
Ça, C'est l'Amour
I Am
(I Never Felt More) Like Falling
    in Love
In the Middle of an Island
No Hard Feelings
One for My Baby
One Kiss Away from Heaven
Sold to the Man with the Broken
    Heart
Weary Blues from Waitin'

1958
Alone at Last
Blue Moon
Crazy Rhythm
Firefly
Love, Look Away
Love Song from Beauty and the
    Beast (Love Me, Love Me,
    Love Me)
Now I Lay Me Down to Sleep
The Beat of My Heart
The Night That Heaven Fell
Young and Warm and Wonderful
You're So Right for Me

1959
Ask Anyone in Love
Being True to One Another
Climb Ev'ry Mountain
It's So Peaceful in the Country
Smile
The Cool School
You Can't Love 'Em All
You'll Never Get Away from Me

1960
Ask Me
Baby, Talk to Me
Follow Me
I'll Bring You a Rainbow
Marriage-Go-Round
Put on a Happy Face
Ramona
Somebody
Till

*Tony Bennett at a Columbia
recording session at CBS 30th
Street Studio, 1957.*

1961
Close Your Eyes
I'm Coming, Virginia
Marry Young
Tender Is the Night
The Best Is Yet to Come
Toot, Toot, Tootsie! (Goodbye)

1962
Candy Kisses
Comes Once in a Lifetime
Have I Told You Lately?
I Left My Heart in San Francisco
I Wanna Be Around
I Will Live My Life for You
Once Upon a Time

1963
Don't Wait Too Long
Limehouse Blues
Spring in Manhattan
The Good Life
The Little Boy
The Moment of Truth
This Is All I Ask
True Blue Lou

1964
A Taste of Honey
It's a Sin to Tell a Lie
The Kid's a Dreamer
Waltz for Debby
When Joanna Loved Me
Who Can I Turn To? (When
    Nobody Needs Me)

1965
Fly Me to the Moon
How Insensitive
I Only Miss Her When I Think
    of Her
If I Ruled the World
Take the Moment
The Best Thing to Be Is a Person
The Brightest Smile in Town
The Shadow of Your Smile
There's a Lull in My Life

1966
A Time for Love
Baby, Dream Your Dream
Country Girl
Georgia Rose
The Very Thought of You
Touch the Earth
What Makes It Happen

1967
Days of Love
For Once in My Life
Keep Smiling at Trouble
Something in Your Smile

1968
A Fool of Fools
Hi-Ho
Hushabye Mountain
My Favorite Things
Sweet Georgie Fame
The Glory of Love
Where Is Love?
Yesterday I Heard the Rain

1969
A Lonely Place
Before We Say Goodbye
Coco
I've Gotta Be Me
Little Green Apples
MacArthur Park
Over the Sun
People
Play It Again, Sam
They All Laughed
What the World Needs Now Is
    Love
Whoever You Are, I Love You

1970
Eleanor Rigby
Everybody's Talkin'
I'll Begin Again
Something
Think How It's Gonna Be

1971
How Beautiful Is Night (With You)
I Do Not Know a Day I Did Not
    Love You
I Want to Be Happy
I'm Losing My Mind
Love Story (Where Do I Begin)
More and More
Remind Me
Somewhere Along the Line
Tea for Two
The Riviera
The Summer Knows
Walkabout

1972
Easy Come, Easy Go
Living Together, Growing
    Together

Tony Bennett, oil painting by Everett Raymond Kinstler, 2014.

Love
Maybe This Time
O Sole Mio
The Good Things in Life
Twilight World

1973
All That Love Went to Waste
Give Me Love, Give Me Peace
I Wish I Were in Love Again
If I Could Go Back
Love Is the Thing
My Love
Some of These Days
Tell Her It's Snowing

1975
Life Is Beautiful
Mr. Magic
One
There'll Be Some Changes Made

1976
There's Always Tomorrow

1990
When Do the Bells Ring?

1993
Steppin' Out
White Christmas

1994
Moonglow (with k.d. lang)

2001
New York State of Mind (with
    Billy Joel)

2002
What a Wonderful World (with
    k.d. lang)

2004
All for You/Time to Smile

2006
Just in Time (with Michael Bublé)

2011
Body and Soul (with Amy
    Winehouse)
The Lady Is a Tramp (with Lady
    Gaga)
Don't Get Around Much
    Anymore (with Michael
    Bublé)

2014
I Can't Give You Anything but
    Love (with Lady Gaga)
Winter Wonderland (with Lady
    Gaga)

INDEX

PICTURE CREDITS